**BDM's PC Knowledge Series**

Windows 10
The Beginners' Guide

From sending emails and chatting on Skype, to customising the Start menu and using Windows Defender, this guide is crammed full of step-by-step guides that are perfect for the new Windows 10 user. Whether you have been using Windows for a while, or if you have just bought your first Windows 10 PC, this guide is full of useful advice, essential tips and all that you need to take your computing knowledge to the next level.

Our step-by-step guides and tutorials make getting the most from your computer easy and there is something new to learn on every page. Including some of the most important elements of Windows 10, and something everyone who uses a computer online should know more about, the security and privacy features. So what are you waiting for? Turn the page and start to build your understanding of Windows 10!

Russ Ware
Editor
Email: russ@bdmpublications.com

BDM's PC Knowledge Series
Windows 10 - The Beginners' Guide
Volume TWENTY - ISSN 2050-9871

Published by: Black Dog Media Limited (BDM)
Editor: Graham Daniels
Art Director & Production: Mark Ayshford
Production Manager: Karl Linstead
Design: Lena Whitaker, Martin Smith
Editorial: Graham Daniels, Russ Ware
Sub Editor: Paul Beard

Printed and bound in Great Britain by: GD Web Offset Ltd

Print Services supplied by: Media First (International) Ltd

Newsstand distribution by:
Seymour Distribution Limited
2, East Poultry Avenue, London EC1A 9PT

International distribution by: Pineapple Media Limited
www.pineapple-media.com

International Licensing:
Black Dog Media has many great publications and all are available for licensing worldwide. For more information go to: www.brucesawfordlicensing.com; email: bruce@brucesawfordlicensing.com telephone: 0044 7831 567372.

BDM's PC Knowledge Series: Windows 10 - The Beginners' Guide is an independent publication and as such does not necessarily reflect the views or opinions of the producers of software, applications or products contained within. This publication is not endorsed or associated in any way with Microsoft or any associate or affiliate company.
All copyrights, trademarks and registered trademarks for the respective computer software and hardware companies are acknowledged.
Assorted images used within this publication are reproduced under licence from Shutterstock.com
Some content may have been published in previous volumes or BDM titles. We advise potential buyers to check the suitability of content prior to purchase. Prices, international availability, ratings, titles and content are subject to change.
All information was correct at time of print.
For all advertising and promotional opportunities please contact: enquiries@bdmpublications.com

 Black Dog Media Limited (BDM)
Registered in England & Wales No: 5311511

Contents
Windows 10 – The Beginners' Guide

6 Get Started with Windows 10

8	Upgrade to Windows 10
10	Set Up a Microsoft Account
12	Creating a Child Account in Windows 10
14	Sign in to Windows 10
16	Choose Sign-in Options
18	Exploring the Windows 10 Settings
20	Updating Windows 10
22	History and Future of Windows 10
24	Windows 10 – Fall Creators and Beyond
26	Exploring Start Menu, Action Center and Taskbar
28	Using the Start Menu
30	Using the Action Center
32	Using the Windows Taskbar
34	Exploring with the File Explorer
36	Using the File Explorer
38	Create and Manage Desktop Folders
40	Using the Task View Feature
42	Using Windows 10 Snap Assist

44 Personalising Windows 10

46	The Essential Guide to Personalisation
54	Using Sticky Notes in Windows 10
56	Installing Alternative Browsers
58	File Associations and Protocols
60	Managing Your Notifications

62 Getting Online with Windows 10

64	Connecting to the Internet
66	Exploring the Edge Browser
68	Using the Edge Browser
72	Searching with Windows 10
74	Using the Cortana Assistant
78	Exploring the Windows 10 Mail App
80	Set Up and Use Email and Accounts

84 Windows 10 Security and Privacy

86	Internet Safety and Security Tips
90	Security Risks for Windows 10 Users
92	Manage Your Privacy Settings
94	Using the Windows Defender Tools
96	Creating Backups of Your Files
98	Back Up with a Recovery Drive
100	How to Use the Dynamic Lock
101	How to Use Night Light Mode
102	Top Ten Antivirus and Security Packages

Contents

104 Windows 10 Apps and Software

106   Exploring the Windows Store
108   Using the Windows Store
110   Exploring the Maps App
112   Navigating with the Maps App
114   Using the People App
116   Exploring the Calendar App
118   Plan Events and Appointments
120   Exploring the Photos App
122   Importing Photos to Your PC
124   Using the Photos App
128   Exploring the Groove Music App
130   Using Groove Music
132   Using the Phone Companion
134   Using Skype in Windows 10

136 Windows 10 Maintenance

138   Using Windows 10 Maintenance Tools
140   Exploring the Task Manager
142   Free Up Storage Space
144   10 Tips to Speed Up Windows 10

6   Get Started with Windows 10

Learn how to get your Windows 10 PC set up properly and make everything that follows easier.

44 Personalising Windows 10

Explore the different ways you can instantly make your copy of Windows 10 perfect for you.

62 Getting Online with Windows 10

Taking your Windows 10 PC online can be as easy as connecting to a network and opening Edge.

84 Windows 10 Security and Privacy

Learn how to spot and avoid security and privacy issues when you are using your Windows PC.

104 Windows 10 Apps and Software

Get to grips with the core Windows 10 apps and software and get the most from your computer.

136 Windows 10 Maintenance

Discover the best ways to keep your Windows 10 PC running smoothly and problem free.

10 **Set Up Your Microsoft Account**

It may seem basic but setting up a user account properly will pay off later.

18 **Exploring Windows 10 Settings**

Learn how to control and manage the operating system through the main settings.

34 **Explore the File Explorer**

Learn how to use and get the most from the improved Windows 10 File Explorer.

Get Started with Windows 10

Give yourself a firm foundation to start from and everything else should be that little bit easier to use and understand. Learn the steps you need to get your PC set up with new user accounts and the all-important Microsoft account; and get to grips with all of the main elements of the Windows 10 desktop, including the brand new Start menu, Action Center and taskbar.

8	Upgrade to Windows 10
10	Set Up a Microsoft Account
12	Creating a Child Account in Windows 10
14	Sign in to Windows 10
16	Choose Sign-in Options
18	Exploring the Windows 10 Settings
20	Updating Windows 10
22	History and Future of Windows 10
24	Windows 10 – Fall Creators and Beyond
26	Exploring Start Menu, Action Center and Taskbar
28	Using the Start Menu
30	Using the Action Center
32	Using the Windows Taskbar
34	Exploring with the File Explorer
36	Using the File Explorer
38	Create and Manage Desktop Folders
40	Using the Task View Feature
42	Using Windows 10 Snap Assist

Upgrade to Windows 10

It's fairly easy to upgrade your older version of Windows to Windows 10. If you have spent any time at all on your computer recently, you will no doubt have seen the pop-up messages urging you to upgrade for free for a limited period. Depending whether you are upgrading from Windows 7 or 8, or an older version such as Vista, the process is slightly different.

Upgrading From Windows 7 or 8

Installing Windows 10 on a Windows 7 or 8.1 PC is a relatively simple process, as long as you follow a few basic rules and ensure that the hardware specification matches with what is required by the newer OS.

Step 1 The first thing you need to do is to make sure you have installed all of the updates for Windows 7 or Windows 8, including update KB3035583 so that you'll receive the "Get Windows 10" app. When you see the message pop-up, click the box and follow the instructions to begin installation.

Step 3 Next you'll be asked to sign in with your Microsoft account. If you have an Outlook.com, Hotmail or Xbox account you can use those details. If you don't have a Microsoft account you can sign up for one. The final part of the account setup process is to choose a password or PIN login.

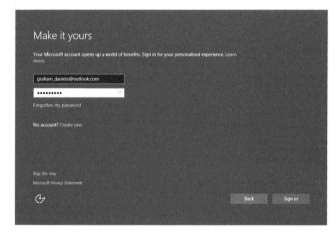

Step 2 Your PC will run through several things during this time, especially checking that everything installed and connected to it is OK with the update. You may be asked to identify whether the PC belongs to a company or if it's a personal PC, depending on the version of Windows being installed.

Step 4 You will now see a series of screens explaining some of the new additions to Windows 10 and be given some choices as to file storage, new apps and how Cortana works. Windows 10 will now set up your new apps and load into the start-up screen. Log in to get going on the new OS.

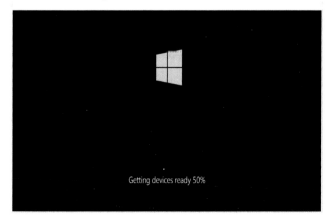

Upgrading From Windows XP or Vista

You can't upgrade Windows to the new version directly from XP or Vista. Be sure to back up your files first or you will lose them.

Step 1 Here we're doing a clean install from a USB drive copy of Windows 10. If you downloaded Windows you'll get some instructions on how to get it to this point. You must ensure that your PC meets the minimum requirements for Windows 10 before installing.

Step 2 Usually your PC will boot from the Windows USB drive without issue, though you may need some additional information on how to boot from a USB drive if it doesn't work. The Windows installation process doesn't look like much but you have to start somewhere.

Step 3 The next screen enables you to select the default language you want to install. Chances are you will also need to enter the product key for Windows at this stage. This will be included in your pack if you bought Windows 10 from a store or you'll have been given it if you downloaded Windows.

Step 4 Like all software, Windows 10 comes with a licence agreement that you'll need to accept. A necessary evil if you like. So tick the box and click Next. It gives you the authority to use the software and terms and conditions of use, and it's a legal agreement from Microsoft's side.

Step 5 You may or may not see this screen during your clean installation of Windows 10. It's likely that if you do, the Upgrade part will be greyed out. We're installing Windows only here, which is referred to as 'Custom'. You'll then be asked which drive you want to install Windows on.

Step 6 When the actual installation process is completed, Windows 10 will begin the set-up process detailed on the previous page, for Windows 7 or 8.1. You'll see several screens inviting you to set up your sign in details and various settings before you get to the new Windows 10 desktop.

Set Up a Microsoft Account

When you sign into Windows 10, you'll be asked whether you want to do so with a Microsoft account. You can still have a local account to use Windows if you wish. You'll also need an account to download from the Windows Store.

Setting Up and Configuring

Microsoft prefers its users to have a single main account. If you don't have a Microsoft account, it's really easy to get one. Here we'll show you how, as well as look at any other further settings you might need.

How to Get a Microsoft Account

Although you can sign up for an account when you install or initialise Windows 10 for the first time, you can also create one at https://account.microsoft.com. This is also where you can customise your account settings, which we'll come onto shortly.

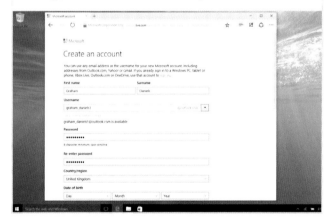

Do You Already Have an Account?

Even if you think you haven't got a Microsoft account, it's quite possible that you do have one. Ever had a Hotmail or Outlook.com address? Or did you use MSN or Windows Live Messenger? You can sign in with those same credentials.

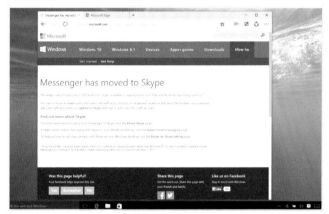

What Does an Account Get You Access to?

As well as Windows and Outlook.com, you can also use your account across all Microsoft services including Xbox Live, Skype, Office and Bing as well as Windows-powered phones (your Contacts are automatically synchronised with your account, too).

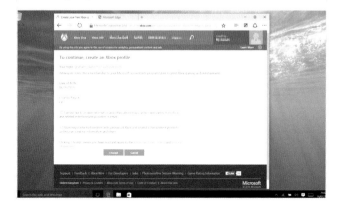

Do You Need an Outlook.com Email Address?

Contrary to popular belief, you can create a Microsoft account with any email address – you don't need to have an Outlook. com (formerly Windows Live Mail and Hotmail) email address. So even if you use Gmail, you can still get a Microsoft account. It's optional whether you have a new Outlook.com email account as well.

How to Sign into Windows with an Account

During the initialisation process for Windows 10, you'll be asked to sign in using your Microsoft account (so don't click Sign in with a Local Account instead). Microsoft will then go and fetch any information connected to your account (such as your profile picture).

Sync Your Settings

In Settings > Accounts > Sync your Settings, you can also tell your PC what details you want it to synchronise to your Microsoft account. A lot of the synchronisations are to do with desktop customisations, but you can also decide whether you want your stored passwords to be synchronised using your account.

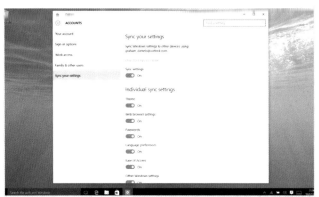

Account Settings

Once you've signed in using your Microsoft account, you can configure your account within Windows 10. Go to the Settings app and choose Accounts. You can change options to do with the account itself here as well as how often your computer should require you to sign in.

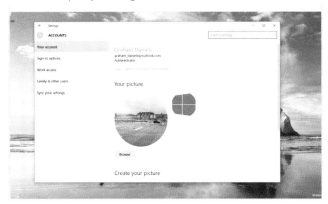

Buy Apps and More

Services within Windows that use your Microsoft account – such as Mail or the Windows Store – will automatically have your account details ready for you. You'll be able to get access to your purchase history and more via the individual apps.

Manage Your Account

Clicking Manage your Account will take you to your account page online. You may see an update to your account terms and conditions when you do this for the first time. Here you can see recent purchases, your devices, personal info (plus payment info) and change your password.

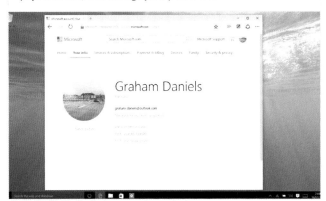

Add Family Members

Also within Settings > Accounts you can add family members to your PC so they use their own login. You don't really want other people using your Microsoft account to sign in. You can specify time limits and restrict the type of games that can be played. You're also able to add people that aren't in your family group.

Creating a Child Account in Windows 10

If you're sharing a Windows 10 computer with your children, or they have one for themselves, then setting them up with their own account will work better for you both in the long run. A Windows 10 child account gives them freedom, whilst allowing you to set up certain restrictions for your own peace of mind.

Windows 10 Child Account

With a Windows 10 child account you're able to set up age restrictions and time limits and ensure they're not visiting sites or using apps they shouldn't.

Step 1 Start off by clicking the Windows Start button and typing 'account'. The first result that should appear is Manage your account, if anything else appears, as in you have some work labelled 'account' or such, then scroll down until you find the Manage your account option.

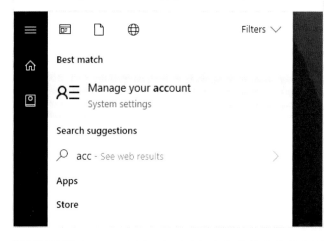

Step 2 You'll now find yourself at the Windows 10 Settings page, in the Accounts section portal. Notice there are links down the left-hand side, look for the Family & Other People link and click it to continue with the process.

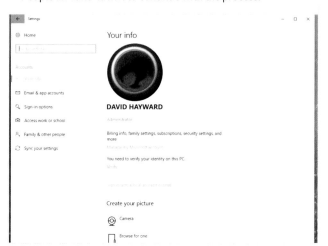

Step 3 You'll need to sign in with a Microsoft account for this to work. If you've not already set up a main Microsoft login account for Windows, you'll need to click the Sign in with a Microsoft account option. Once done, you'll be presented with the current family members who already have MS accounts.

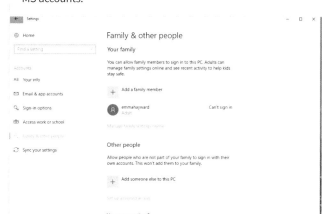

Step 4 Next, click on the Add a Family Member link, by the plus sign under the Your Family section. This will launch a new pop-up window to create a new Microsoft account. You need to make sure that your child has an email address and that you or they can currently access it to authenticate the process.

Step 5 Click the Add a Child option in the new account window and enter their email in the text box section below. When you're ready, click on the Next button.

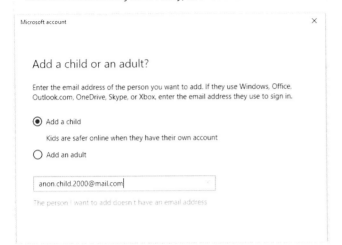

Step 6 You'll now get the message that it's not a Microsoft account, click the link to Create a Microsoft Account. This will bring you to a new window with the email address you've entered already filled in. Complete the relevant details and click the Next button to continue.

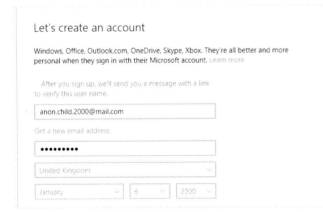

Step 7 The next section details what level of search and advertising Microsoft will allow to the account. Obviously you can untick both boxes, or leave them as they are, depending on what you want. However, for the sake of enhanced privacy, we recommend unticking both. Click Next when you're ready.

Step 8 The child's account is now ready to be activated. The message box informs you that you'll need to respond to the email Microsoft has sent before they're able to login in to the Windows 10 computer. Click the Close button when you're ready.

Step 9 Microsoft will send some emails to the child's account. One will be a Verification email, which you, or your child, will need to click the link to activate the account. They need to login to Microsoft online to complete the process. The other email will be an invitation to join the family account, which you also need to Accept.

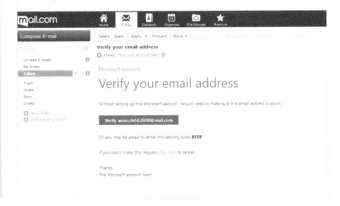

Step 10 Using the child account to join the family will send emails to you confirming the accepted invitation. Back at the Windows 10 Family & Other People window, you can now click the child's account and allow it to login; or manage it via the Microsoft Family portal online, which we'll look at in the next tutorial.

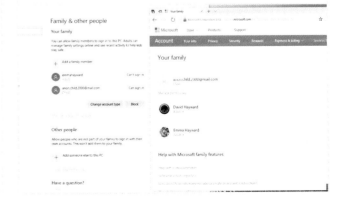

Sign in to Windows 10

Whether you install Windows yourself or initialise it on a new PC, you'll want to sign into it using a Microsoft account. This means your settings can be synchronised across your PCs. One great use for this is wireless network settings.

Signing In Using Your Microsoft Account

We'll look at how you can sign in when you're installing Windows 10. And also how to register your details and add a Microsoft account if you're already using Windows 10. An essential, but unexciting part of the setup process.

Make It Yours During the Windows 10 installation process you'll be asked to sign into Windows. Now, you can skip this step should you wish to, but we'd recommend you don't. You'll need to use your Microsoft account to download apps and settings (such as new printers) and synchronise your network settings between PCs automatically.

Sign Up If you use Xbox or used Hotmail or Windows Live, you should be able to sign in with those details. During the Windows 10 installation you can sign up for a Microsoft account if you don't already have one. Just fill in your name, existing email address (you can sign up for a new Outlook.com one should you wish) as well as your location.

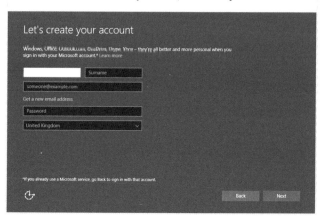

Make Changes Your Microsoft account replaces the old way to sign into Windows, with a simple username (and possibly a password). You can still sign in that way - that's what we've done here to show you that it can be done - but it's not recommended. You can make changes in Settings > Accounts.

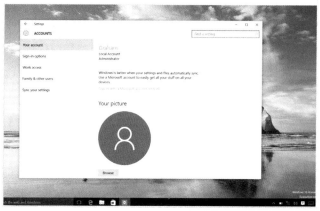

Signing In We're now going to show you how to replace the old-style sign-in process with your Microsoft account should you be using Windows in this way. Note we didn't have an account picture in the previous step. Now click Sign in with a Microsoft Account instead. You'll then see this window prompting you to wait a second.

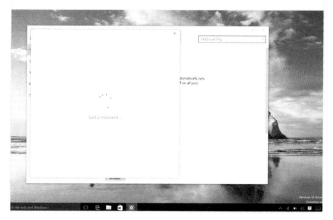

Enter Your Details

Enter your Microsoft account username and password here. Much like during the Windows installation process, you can choose to create a new Microsoft account at this stage with any existing email address (once again, you can also sign up for a new Outlook.com one). Then click Sign in.

Authenticate Your Device

If you have a mobile number associated with your Microsoft account, you may see this security step. You'll firstly be asked to enter the last four digits of your mobile phone number. If you do this correctly, Microsoft will then text you a code. Click Next to move on.

Enter the Code

The code you receive by text will be unique to you – enter it here and click Next. More companies are relying on our phones as a way to confirm identity; you can also do this with other major online account providers such as Google or Facebook. It's called two-step authentication.

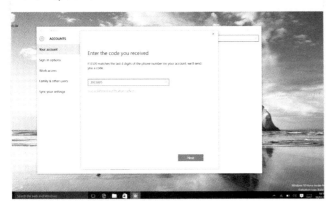

Beyond Passwords

Windows 10 also introduces some new ways to authenticate who you are and sign you into Windows. Expect to see facial recognition play more of a part in future, but for now, you'll be offered a PIN to sign into Windows rather than your Microsoft account password. Click PIN Me if you want to do this.

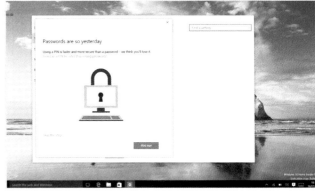

Confirm Your Password

The great advantage of using a PIN rather than a password is that it is usually a lot faster to type it in. It's also a lot better for touch devices. Before you choose your PIN you'll be asked to confirm your password again.

Choose Your PIN

Finally, choose your PIN. Windows wants to be more phone-like in terms of usability, and using a PIN is one way it's evolving along these lines. After all, many of us are already used to unlocking our mobile phones in this way.

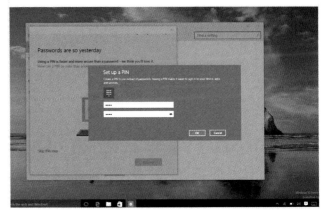

Choose Sign-in Options

New technologies inside Windows 10 enable you to log in with a fingerprint reader if you have one and – in the future – you'll be able to use facial recognition too. But you can still set up a picture password or PIN to make logging in easier.

The Various Ways You can Log into Windows 10

Whether you use a password, PIN, picture password or fingerprint to log into Windows 10 we've got you covered. Let's take a look at the different ways available to sign in to Windows 10, from the least to the most secure.

What You See When you start-up Windows 10, you'll see the lock screen. If you used Windows 8, it's something you'll be familiar with. You can get other information displayed here including network and battery life information, and you can change what appears in Settings > Personalisation > Lock Screen.

Facial Recognition If you've seen adverts for Windows 10, you'll have seen that it makes a big play of not needing your password to log in. The catch is that you need a special Intel RealSense camera to use facial recognition. Laptops will have this built-in, but few do as yet.

Log into Windows As soon as you click any key or tap on the lock screen you'll get this – the Windows logon screen. You can use your password, fingerprint reader, picture password or PIN if you've set one up. Here a PIN is our default, but you can always use the Sign in Options button to use a different method providing it's set up on your PC.

Verifying Identity Future devices will be able to recognise who we are. This is an image of a demo from Microsoft, but it shows how our identity could be verified by our device's camera for financial transactions, logging into websites and much more. This technology – along with the ability to log in using your fingerprint - is referred to as Windows Hello by Microsoft.

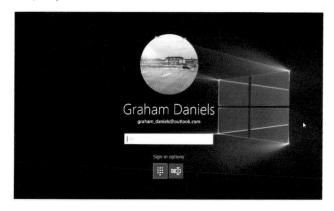

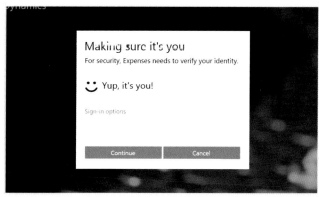

Sign-in Settings

You'll find the settings that govern logging into Windows in the Accounts section of the Settings app. Here you can set up your PIN should you choose to, or set up a picture password. It's this latter option we'll look at setting up for much of the remainder of this tutorial.

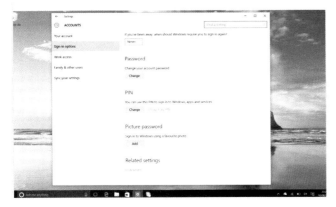

Set Up a Fingerprint Reader

If your PC has a fingerprint reader or compatible RealSense camera, you'll see extra options in this Settings screen under Windows Hello. Click the Set Up button to get started with these and you'll run through a setup wizard. Next, we'll show you how to set up a picture password.

Your Password

As with every time you set up a new way to log into Windows, you'll be asked to provide your password. Passwords don't go away completely even if you specify a new way to log in; you'll still need it to log onto Windows services online, for example.

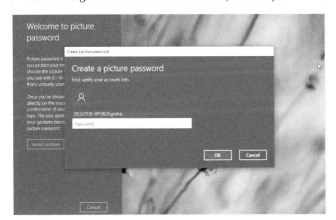

What is a Picture Password?

A picture password can be used with a mouse or touchscreen, but it comes into its own when used with the latter. That's because it uses particular gestures to identify you and this isn't the easiest thing to do with the mouse. You define these gestures by 'drawing' them on top of a picture.

Any Image

You can use any image you choose, as you can see, we've changed from the default option in the previous slide. Next you need to do three gestures on this image, so we did one following the shape of the landscape and another couple following the shape of the green light.

Confirm and Finish

Once you've performed your gestures, you need to confirm them by drawing them once more with your finger. Some people find this a bit difficult, but once you get the hang of it, you'll be fine. If you're worried about being locked out of your PC then don't be – remember, you're always able to use your password or PIN as well.

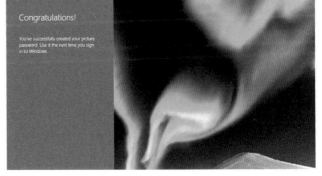

Exploring the Windows 10 Settings

Windows 10 settings are actually spread across a couple of different menus but the main settings can be accessed by clicking the Start menu button, where you should see them pinned in the folder list. If not you can search for 'Settings' using the Windows 10 search bar. You can pin the settings icon to the taskbar or Start menu for easier access.

External Device Settings

This is where you come to manage all of your connected devices, from printers and scanners to your mouse and keyboard. Related settings are also found here, including Bluetooth, and touchpad settings if you are using a laptop.

Main System Settings

Here you can find settings and options for things like the Display, Notifications, Apps, Power and Storage. The 'About' section contains lots of information about the hardware in your computer as well as the operating system software version being used.

Account Settings

Account settings contains all of the options you need for managing your local Microsoft account. This includes the secure sign-In options such as password, PIN and picture password, as well as the new Dynamic Lock settings, workplace or school access settings and Microsoft Family settings.

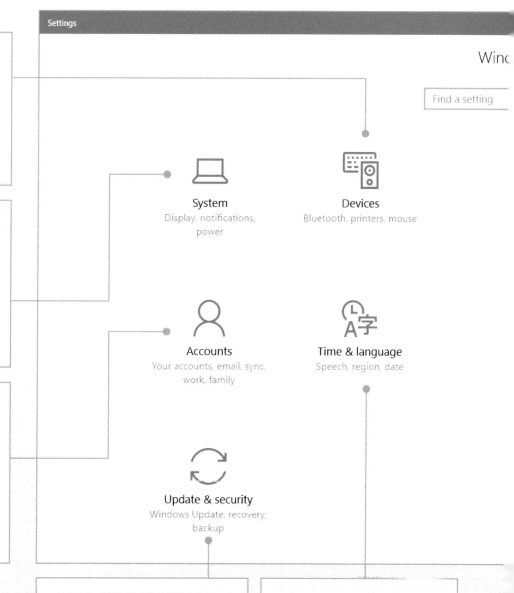

Settings

Wind

Find a setting

System
Display, notifications, power

Devices
Bluetooth, printers, mouse

Accounts
Your accounts, email, sync, work, family

Time & language
Speech, region, date

Update & security
Windows Update, recovery, backup

Update and Security Settings

It is important to make sure that your Windows computer is up to date with all the latest updates and revisions. Within this settings menu, you can check to see which updates are available to download and install. You can also create backups and recovery discs here.

Time & Language Settings

As well as the obvious settings for the time and date displayed on your computer (having this information correct is more important than many think) this is where you come to change the display and input language for your computer.

Network & Internet Settings

If you are having problems with your Internet connection, this is where you should come to find details and information. Everything from Internet options to flight mode and firewall settings can be found here. Each section contains links to more advanced options.

PIN THE SETTINGS

To pin the settings icon to the taskbar, click on the Start menu and then right click on the Settings icon (the cog-shaped icon) and choose 'More…' Then choose 'Pin to Taskbar'. The Settings icon will now permanently appear in the bar at the bottom of the screen.

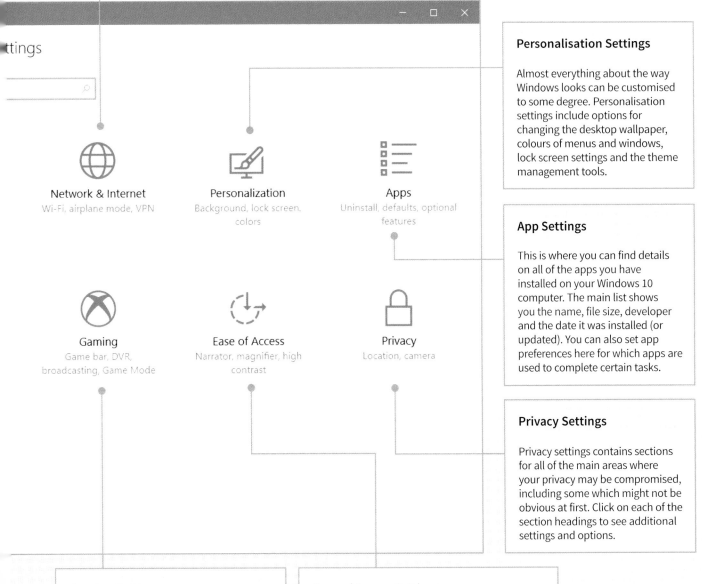

ttings

Network & Internet
Wi-Fi, airplane mode, VPN

Personalization
Background, lock screen, colors

Apps
Uninstall, defaults, optional features

Gaming
Game bar, DVR, broadcasting, Game Mode

Ease of Access
Narrator, magnifier, high contrast

Privacy
Location, camera

Personalisation Settings

Almost everything about the way Windows looks can be customised to some degree. Personalisation settings include options for changing the desktop wallpaper, colours of menus and windows, lock screen settings and the theme management tools.

App Settings

This is where you can find details on all of the apps you have installed on your Windows 10 computer. The main list shows you the name, file size, developer and the date it was installed (or updated). You can also set app preferences here for which apps are used to complete certain tasks.

Privacy Settings

Privacy settings contains sections for all of the main areas where your privacy may be compromised, including some which might not be obvious at first. Click on each of the section headings to see additional settings and options.

Gaming Settings

A new addition to the settings with the recent update, here you will find the newly added gaming tools. These include a game recorder (Game DVR), the tools for broadcasting your games and the Game Mode option. This helps to optimise any games you play on your PC.

Ease of Access Settings

Previously called Accessibility. If you have additional accessibility needs to use a computer efficiently, you can find lots of settings here to make life easier. From a Narrator tool and screen magnifier, to closed captioning and mouse and keyboard settings. You can even make the cursor thicker and easier to see

Updating Windows 10

Keeping your Windows 10 computer up to date is important for many reasons. First, major updates, such as the Anniversary update, will add major new features that you shouldn't miss out on. Second, all updates are there for a reason, usually to fix problems, close security holes and add improvements.

Checking for Updates

If you think that your PC needs to be updated, you don't need to wait for the automatic update process to kick in. You can quite easily check for updates yourself.

Step 1 You can find the Windows 10 update information in the main settings app. Tap the Windows key or click the Start menu button and then select the Settings icon from the side of the menu. Click the "Updates & Security" heading in the menu to open the relevant settings screen.

Step 2 At the top of the window you should immediately see a message telling you whether Windows 10 is up to date or if updates are currently available. Directly below this message is a button labelled "Check for updates". Even if the message says up to date, it is worth clicking this button.

Step 3 Any available updates will now display at the top of the window and the Check button will change to an Install button. You can install the updates straight away, but you will need to restart your PC after the install is complete, or you can reschedule to a more convenient time.

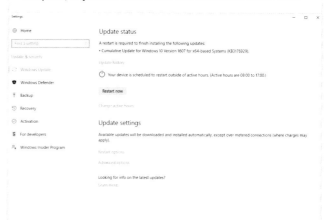

Step 4 If you want to check which updates have been installed, perhaps if you need to confirm a security update for work, you can easily do so by clicking the "Update History" link directly below the check for updates button. Updates are displayed, with more info available by clicking.

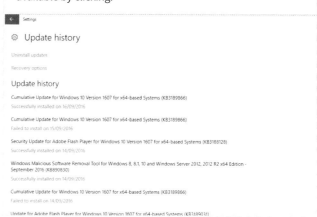

Windows Update Settings

There are several additional and advanced options available which can make the whole update process quicker, easier and more efficient, which is always a good thing.

Active Hours By setting your active hours, you can tell your computer when you will most likely be using it. If you have updates set to automatically install and restart, they will only do so outside of your active hours. Useful for ensuring updates don't lose you school or office work.

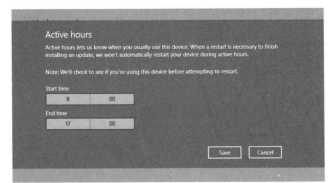

Automatic Set Up Some updates require you to restart your PC and sign in to Windows in order to finish installing the update. Windows 10 can help prevent this from happening by allowing Windows to use your sign in info to create a special token. Go to Advanced update options > Use my sign-in info...

Custom Restart Time When a restart is scheduled, this option is available to temporarily override active hours and schedule a custom time to finish installing the current update. You will still need to make sure your device is plugged in at the scheduled time.

Uninstall Updates If for some reason you need to uninstall a particular update, perhaps the update is causing some software to not behave properly, you can do so fairly easily. From the Updates windows, click Update History > Uninstall Updates and use the interface to remove the update.

Update Delivery You can choose how Windows updates are delivered in the Advanced Options. Windows Update Delivery Optimisation lets you get Windows updates and Windows Store apps from sources in addition to Microsoft. This can help you get updates and apps more quickly.

Windows Insider As a beginner, you probably aren't too worried about seeing updates before they are released to the general public but this is exactly what the Windows Insider program lets you do. By joining the Insider program, you are potentially helping in the development of Windows 10 and beyond.

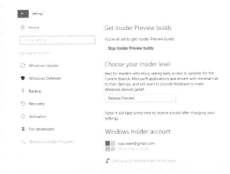

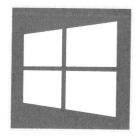

Exploring Start Menu, Action Center and Taskbar

The Start menu, taskbar and Action Center are likely to be three of the most used areas of the Windows 10 interface for most people. There have been several additions and improvements to these tools in the recent Anniversary update, making them even easier and more intuitive to use, so let's take a look at what you can do with these essential Windows tools.

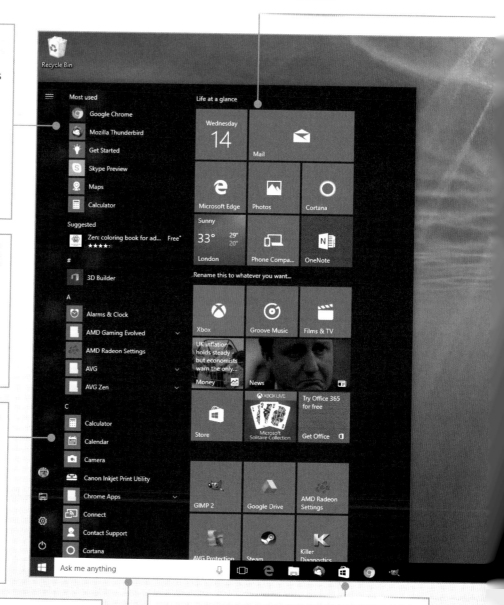

All Apps List

As you use Windows 10 and the various apps and software, a list of your most used tools will appear here. This is constantly updated as your use of the OS evolves. At the top of the All Apps list is a Recently Added section, showing newly installed software and a Most Used section showing your favourite applications. Click either heading to open a jump to letter menu.

System Folders

You can change the folders that appear in the bottom half of the Start menu, depending on how you use Windows 10. Settings, Power and All Apps will always be present in this part of the menu but everything else can be chosen in Settings > Personalisation.

Start Menu Folders

If you pin apps to the Start menu, their icons will appear below the block of tiles. You can now move these app icons into folders within the Start menu. To do this, click and drag one icon on top of another. If the bottom icon expands slightly rather than moving out of the way, drop the icon to create the folder.

Search Bar

The search bar is always visible to the right of the Windows button, unless viewing an app or game in full screen mode. Click in the Ask me Anything box and the search window will open. You can either type your search term or, if set up, use the Mic to ask Cortana. When the search menu opens, it will hopefully be prefilled with relevant information and links.

Taskbar (left)

The taskbar contains shortcuts to many of the most commonly used apps, including the Edge browser, App Store and File Explorer. You can add any app to the taskbar by right-clicking on the tile or app icon and selecting Pin to taskbar from the menu. Right-clicking on the taskbar will also allow you to add different toolbars to it.

PERSONALISATION

You can personalise the Start menu and taskbar in a number of ways. Open the main settings and click on Personalisation. In the Start section you will see sliders to control whether you see recently added apps, most used apps, etc. You can also set the Start menu to display in full screen like it did in Windows 8.1.

Start Menu Tiles

Just as with Windows 8.1, the tiles that appear in the Start menu display information (when appropriate) from the apps and services they link to. You can customise the look of the tiles by right-clicking on them and selecting an option from the menu that appears. Tiles are now automatically split into relevant sections, e.g. Play and Explore.

Action Center Notifications

Notifications in the Action Center range from security alerts and system errors, to emails and Facebook updates. If you are seeing notifications here that you don't need, Twitter updates for example, you can right-click the heading and turn off notifications for that app.

Quick Settings

The Quick Settings displayed here will vary depending on the device you are using. You will normally see Wi-Fi, Note, All Settings, Bluetooth, Location and Quiet Hours here at the very least. If the Quick Settings menu is collapsed, click the Expand button to show the full menu. You can now customise the Quick Settings buttons shown in Settings > System > Notifications and Actions.

Taskbar (right)

The right-hand side of the taskbar contains several essential Windows tools. Here you can check battery power (if using a laptop), your Wi-Fi connection details, speaker volume and several other things. You will also find the button to open the new Action Center here. The Anniversary update added notification badges here, so you can see unread notification amounts at a glance.

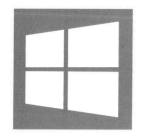

Using the Start Menu

The Start menu in Windows 10 is about much more than just displaying a list of your apps and software. It includes Live Tiles, shortcuts to folders and settings, and you can now even create folders within the menu itself. So whether you just want to use it as a simple list or if you want to make it the hub of your PC, the Start menu has it covered.

Get to Grips with Start

Microsoft has completely redesigned the Start menu for a new era and it seems to get improved with every update to the OS, so it takes a little getting used to at first. Here's our tour of the new Start.

Step 1   You open the Start menu by clicking the Windows icon in the bottom left of the desktop or by pressing the Windows key on your keyboard. The menu in Windows 10 is a mix of the Windows 7 and 8 styles but works better than either, with a list of apps on the left and Live Tiles on the right.

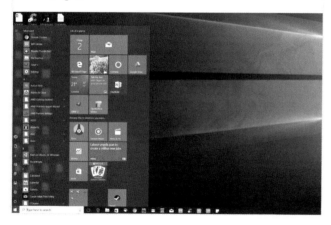

Step 3   You can right-click anything in the live tiles area of the Start menu to bring up the tile menu. This lets you resize, unpin and even turn the live tile into a static tile. There are up to four different sizes of live tile: small, medium, wide and large, giving you lots of ways to build the perfect Start menu.

Step 2   The live tiles work in the same way as they did in Windows 8. You can drag any of them around the menu should you wish to reorder them. You can right-click any file, folder or app in Windows 10 and select Pin to Start to include it here. Once in the menu, click and drag to rearrange tiles.

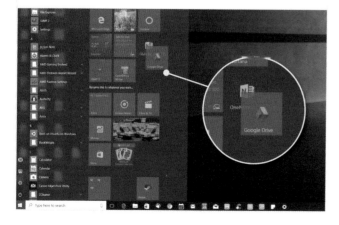

Step 4   The tiles are split into groups. You can click the headings on existing groups to rename them. Dragging one of the tiles to the bottom of the menu, to an unused area of the menu, enables you to create a new group. A bar will appear at the bottom to indicate that a new group will be created.

Step 5 The Start menu now allows for the creation of folders. This means that you can further organise the menu by keeping related app icons in a single place. To create a folder, simply click and drag an app icon over another. The icon beneath will expand slightly. Drop the dragged icon and the folder is created.

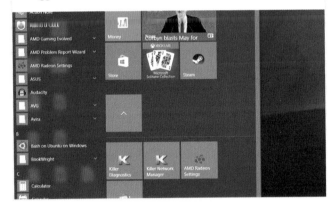

Step 6 On the left-hand side at the bottom, there's a list of key items, such as the Settings app and a shortcut to the File Explorer. Click the power icon and you can shut down or restart your PC. You can add more options to this shortcut section in Settings > Personalisation > Start > Choose which folders appear.

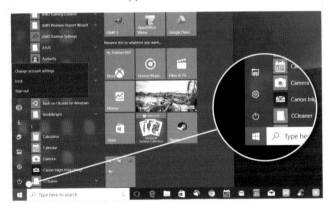

Step 7 The final area of the Start menu is the apps and software list. This displays all of the installed apps and software on your computer (software which doesn't require installation to run won't be shown here). Scroll up and down to view the full list and click the arrow next to apps to see more options.

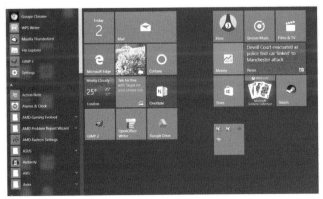

Step 8 The Most Used section at the top of the list enables you to access recently opened programs. This will also show recently opened files, so if you have Microsoft Word installed, simply go to the menu next to the icon in the most used apps menu and you can instantly open your recently worked upon files.

Step 9 Clicking on any of the headings (including the individual letters) of the apps list will open an A-Z selection menu. You can then quickly click on any of the letters to skip directly to the listed apps that begin with that letter, rather than having to scroll down through the entire thing.

Step 10 Finally, Windows 10 also makes it easy to resize the Start menu. Move the mouse to the edges and resize handles will appear, so you can have it covering half your screen or a much smaller proportion. You can even set the Start menu to open full screen, by going to Settings > Personalisation > Start.

Using the Action Center

There have always been pop-up messages in Windows. But now there's a centralised way in which these are treated. Called Action Center (but titled simply 'Notifications'), it's actually designed to be a direct equivalent of the same menu on the Windows Phone.

Make the Most of the Action Center

The new Action Center is a key interface element in Windows which provides you with many switch-on, switch-off options. It's influenced by smartphone and tablet interface designs and really comes into its own in Tablet Mode.

Step 1 The bottom right corner of Windows' desktop taskbar takes on new significance within Windows 10 thanks to a special area for notifications called the Action Center. Hover over the Action Center button and it will tell you if you have any new notifications.

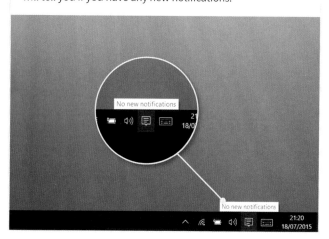

Step 2 This is what the Action Center looks like when you click the button. As you can see, notifications are grouped by app – which apps are listed changes depending on which apps have sent you a notification. Older notifications are greyed out if you have already seen them but not dismissed them.

Step 3 The most powerful part of this pop-up bar is actually at the bottom. This is the new equivalent of the Windows 8 Charms bar and enables you to perform some key functions (or actions). You can expand or collapse this bar depending on the functions you need to access.

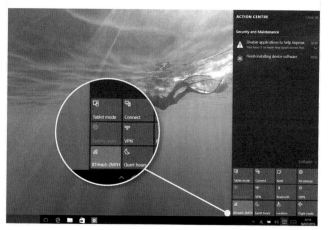

Step 4 Clicking a notification will take you to the app which generated that notification – here we've clicked on a Windows Update notification and the notification has now disappeared. But you might find yourself taken to a file or folder if appropriate.

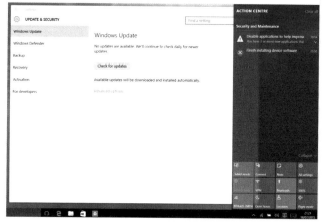

Action Center

Step 5 Clicking on the appropriate charm/action at the bottom of the Action Center app will enable the appropriate setting – here we've unclicked Bluetooth and Location. The latter enables us to control whether our Windows device shares its location with apps as well as with Windows itself for things such as weather updates.

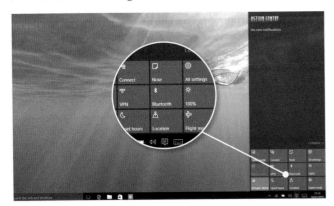

Step 6 Whether you're on a Windows tablet or laptop, at some point you'll either take it on an aircraft or you'll want to shut down the Wi-Fi and Bluetooth on your device to save power. Clicking the Flight mode switches off all wireless communication and places an aeroplane icon in your notifications area instead of the Wi-Fi signal icon.

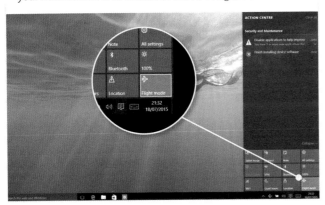

Step 7 Tablet mode is another function you can control from the buttons at the bottom of Action Center. Tablet mode automatically prepares the desktop for use with a touchscreen and your fingers – so the Start menu automatically becomes a Windows 8-style Start screen, the search bar disappears and so on.

Step 8 Switching back shrinks the Start menu once again. Tablet mode should trigger automatically on devices with a detachable keyboard when you undock the keyboard – we'll talk more about Tablet mode later on. You always retain manual control, however.

Step 9 Notifications are very useful, but can be a distraction sometimes; say if you need to concentrate on a particular task or you're in a meeting. To stop distractions during this time you can click the Quiet Hours button in Action Center. No notifications will appear and the Notifications icon changes.

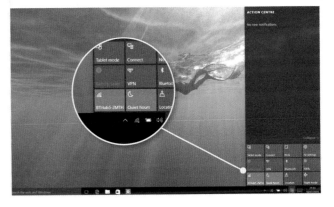

Step 10 When you're done with the notifications on the menu, you can click the Clear All button at the top to dismiss them (see previous step). In Settings > System > Notifications and Actions, you can choose the Quick Actions that appear at the top of the bottom panel in the Action Center.

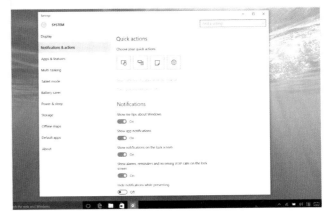

Using the Windows Taskbar

The taskbar has certainly undergone a revival since its relegation in preference of the Start screen in Windows 8. Although it was still present in Windows 8's desktop view, it was definitely second best. Now it's back where it belongs, at the epicentre of Windows. There are a few slight tweaks in the Anniversary update, making it an even more useful tool now.

Mastering the Windows 10 Taskbar

The taskbar has always been more useful than many users realise, and with Windows 10 there are several new features and options which make it even more so. Let's take a look at some of the most important.

Welcome to Windows Windows 10's taskbar is more powerful than ever as you're about to find out. It's now more integrated with the Start menu than before, so if you open Start and start typing, the search bar on the taskbar comes alive, rather than being separate within the Start menu.

Using Jump Lists Right-clicking anything on the taskbar once again brings up a context menu. Apps such as Word and Excel feature jump lists, showing you recent files that you can pin to the list using the drawing pin icon. What appears in the jump list varies between apps. Here, File Explorer shows your recently accessed locations.

Search For It We've covered Windows 10's search features in more detail elsewhere but thanks to our mobile phones there's no denying that we're more used to searching for files, folders and settings rather than having to browse for them. Windows 10 reflects this with a flexible search feature that's also a great way to launch apps.

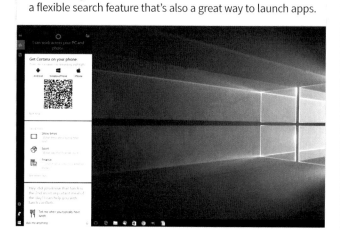

Window Previews Hovering over any open app icon in the taskbar brings up this live preview of the window. If a movie is playing, for example, you'll see it playing here too. If you mouse over the preview, the X icon appears so you can close the window down directly from the taskbar should you wish to.

Task View

The simple white outline icon next to the search bar is Task View. This is Windows 10's brand new way to switch between open apps and it's rather good, providing you can get used to using it. You can also open the Task View by pressing the Windows Key + Tab. Hide the icon by right-clicking on the taskbar and disabling in the menu.

Power and Brightness

If we were using a laptop here rather than a desktop, a battery icon would appear in the notifications area. There's also a link to further settings, taking you to the appropriate area of the all new Settings app. The exact icons that appear here will vary depending on your system set up and apps installed.

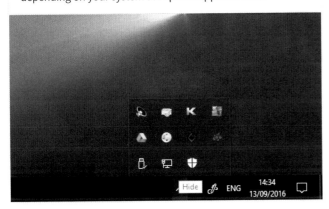

Other Adjustments

You're also able to alter the brightness of your laptop screen as well as enable Power Saving mode by clicking on the battery icon. The volume control next to it features this simple slider but no other settings. You need to right-click to alter other sound settings such as the sound output you wish to select.

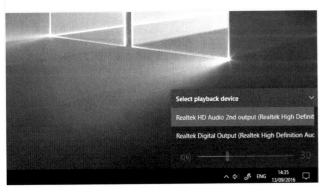

Action Center

This is the another key control area of Windows 10. It gathers together all your pop-up notifications from things like the email app or Windows update. It also features Quick Settings buttons for things like Wi-Fi. The Anniversary update added notification badges, meaning you can see how many unread notifications you have more easily.

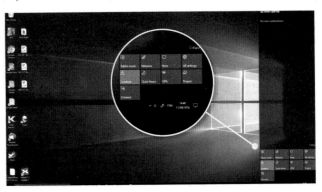

Taskbar Calendar

Click the clock in the taskbar and a small calendar readout appears. The Anniversary update improved this, connecting it to your main Windows Calendar app (for some strange reason it wasn't previously) and this now shows upcoming events you have added. You can hide the Agenda readout using the button at the bottom.

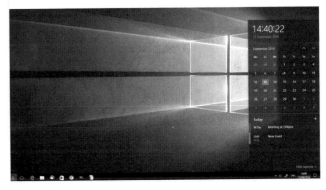

Taskbar Menu

There is still a right-click menu to change taskbar settings; make sure you right-click on an unused area of the taskbar. You can lock the bar, as well as change how the search bar displays. You can make it just a button, like the one in Tablet mode, should you wish to.

Exploring with the File Explorer

Although the File Explorer is much the same as it was in previous versions of Windows, it is still worth exploring it a bit more. The File Explorer is one of the most overlooked tools in Windows but if you want to be able to find your accumulated photos, music files, word documents and other files without having to use Search every time, it is definitely something you should be familiar with.

File Explorer Toolbar

This tabbed toolbar contains all of the tools you need to manage the different files and folders you can view. The main tab is Home, which contains tools for pinning to the Quick Access pane in the Start menu, copying, pasting, moving and renaming files. Once you have selected a file or folder in the main pane, the tools become active.

Navigation Pane - Folders

The left-hand sidebar contains a list of different file folders on your computer. Clicking on any of the folders shown here will display the various files and folders inside, in the main pane. The list is split into sections, including Quick Access/Recent, OneDrive and This PC. If you right-click on a blank area, you can choose to show All Folders here.

Info Bar

The thin bar along the bottom of the File Explorer displays several bits of useful information. If nothing in the main window is selected, the info bar shows the total number of items in the selected folder. Click on a file and the file size is also shown here. If you select several files, the number of items selected is shown, along with the total size of all selected items combined.

THE VIEW TAB

The View tab in the File Explorer allows you to completely change how the window looks, how files are displayed and even whether each item has a permanent check box next to it. One of the most useful tools in the View tab is the Details Pane button. This switches the Preview Pane to show a list of file details instead. This is particularly useful if you are looking at images.

SHOW LIBRARIES

Your Libraries in Windows 10 are preset system folders that are the default locations for your Camera Roll, Music, Saved Pictures, Documents, Pictures and Videos. You can easily have these displayed in the File Explorer. Right-click on any free area of the Navigation Pane and from the menu, click Show Libraries. You can then expand the list of libraries by clicking the small arrow.

Window Controls

Almost every window that opens in Windows includes these controls. From left to right they are: Minimise, Maximise and Close. Just below the standard window controls is a small arrow and a question mark. The arrow is used to show and hide the File Explorer toolbar, which is useful for smaller displays. The question mark will, when clicked, open a help page.

Preview Pane

If the preview pane is enabled, approximately a third of the File Explorer window and indeed, any other folder that you open will be reserved for a preview of any selected files. Normally, only image, html and text files will display a preview in this pane. The preview pane can be increased or decreased in size by clicking and dragging the scroll bar to the left of it.

Folder View

The two buttons here let you choose between viewing the contents of the folder in a thumbnail format or alternatively, as a list. When the folder items are displayed as a list, you can choose to display a varying amount of information, including date last modified, file type and file size. Items shown as a list will still display a preview in the Preview Pane when selected.

Folder Contents Pane

When a folder is selected in the File Location sidebar, its contents are shown in the main pane. The contents of any single folder may vary greatly of course but Windows uses standard icons to show Word documents, text files, various different image formats and shortcuts to apps and software. As you can see here, images will usually be displayed as a thumbnail unless view settings have been changed.

Using the File Explorer

Here we'll take you through the improvements to the general Windows 10 file browser. Many features remain from Windows 7 and 8 (such as clicking in the far right of the taskbar to minimise everything) and apps on the taskbar work the same.

What's New in File Explorer

File Explorer is a much undervalued part of Windows. And while it hasn't fundamentally changed for several versions of the operating system, Windows 10 introduces some interesting enhancements, which we'll take you through here.

Step 1 The way you browse files in Windows 10 is broadly similar to previous versions of Windows, but File Explorer has been enhanced. The main Quick Access window shows you your most frequently used folders (after all, how many of us dip into more than five or ten folders in a day?) and also recent files.

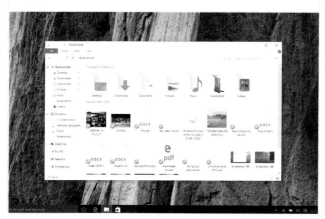

Step 2 The sidebar also works on the same principle and via a new Quick Access feature you can pin folders or files that you want to stick around. It will also show you Frequent folders too. You can pin things permanently onto Quick Access by right-clicking them and selecting Add to Quick Access.

Step 3 There are also new icons across all File Explorer views, while there are a lot more file operations that you can access on the menu at the top of the window (known as the 'ribbon' in Microsoft speak) without the need to use the right-click menu. This is to make it easier for PCs with touchscreens.

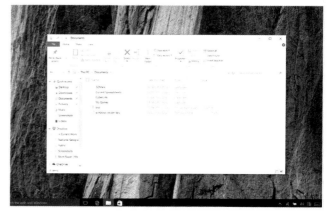

Step 4 This PC is similar to before, but the link to Control Panel has been replaced by the Settings app, which you can now see on the menu bar. Although the Control Panel is still present in the background of Windows 10, Microsoft intends for you to use the new Settings app and directs you there wherever possible.

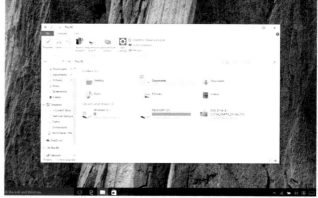

Step 5 Also from This PC (you might know it as My Computer if you previously used an older version of Windows), you can access the Programs and Features Control Panel area if you want to uninstall something.

Step 6 File Explorer's Share tab also gets a new treatment, with the Share logo (first introduced with Windows 8's Charm bar) now used for file sharing from all apps. You can choose to email a file straight from the File Explorer window, add it to a zip file or share it with other Windows users.

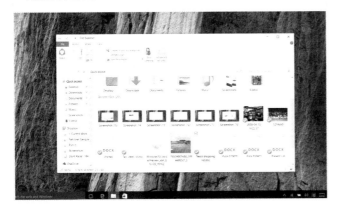

Step 7 If you want to see what other options you have for sharing – perhaps using the Windows Mail app - highlight the files you want to share, then click Share. A pop-up bar will appear on the left of the screen and will show you the options you have to share that file(s) or folder(s).

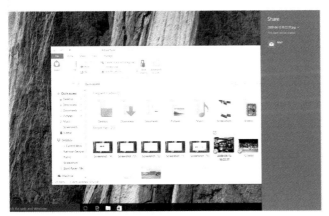

Step 8 The Windows 8 Charm bar has been abandoned in Windows 10 and the functions for Windows Store apps are hidden away inside the apps themselves; functions such as the Settings for the app itself and the ability to Print or Share.

Step 9 If you've come from an earlier version of Windows, you might not be familiar with OneDrive. It's Microsoft's cloud storage application and it's available right from File Explorer in Windows 10, so you can access your files just as if they were on your own computer.

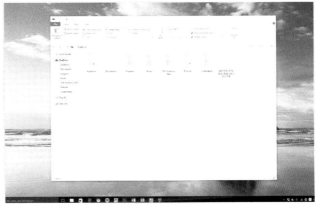

Step 10 On-screen notifications have changed in Windows 10. Unlike in Windows 8, where they display in the top right of the screen, all notification action is now centred around the bottom right. There's also a place where notifications reside after they've popped up.

Create and Manage Desktop Folders

Despite all of the new improvements to Windows over the years, folders have remained as one of the core tools you can use to organise your files. Folders are much more than just boxes to keep your photos or music files in and learning how to make the best use of them can really improve how you use Windows on a day-to-day basis.

Creating New Folders

It may sound too simple if you are a long time Windows user but here's a look at how to create new folders on the desktop and within other folders.

Step 1 On the desktop, right-click and select New folder from the action menu that appears. The familiar yellow folder icon will then appear at that position on the desktop (wherever you clicked), with the name automatically set as 'New folder' but highlighted ready to change.

Step 2 You can leave the name as 'New folder' if you wish. If you then create a second folder next to the first, it will automatically be named 'New folder (2)'. You can rename a folder at any time by left-clicking on the title once, or right-clicking and selecting Rename from the menu.

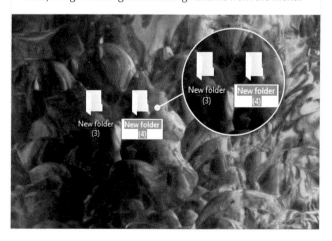

Step 3 Double-click any folder to open it and view the contents. You can move items into a folder by selecting, dragging and dropping into an open folder or a closed one. If the folder is closed, drag the selected items over the top of it until the folder is highlighted, then release.

Step 4 To delete a folder, right-click on it and select Delete from the action menu. You can also click and drag the folder to the Recycle Bin icon on your desktop. Anything in the folder will also be placed in the recycle bin. To move folders around the desktop, just click, drag and drop them.

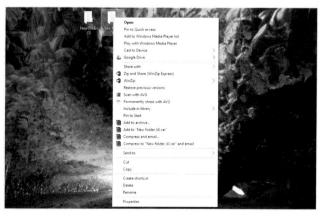

Managing Your Folders

Once created, folders can be adapted and customised in a number of ways. You can even change the default icon used whenever a new folder is added.

Step 1
You can manage a folder in a number of ways without even opening it. Right-click on any folder and the action menu appears. The exact options that appear will depend on the apps or software you have installed but can include scan for viruses, compress, shred, zip and more.

Step 2
The standard (Windows 10) options in the folder action menu include Pin to Quick Access, Open, Share With, Pin to Start, Send To, Cut, Copy and Create Shortcut. If there is a small arrow next to an option in the menu, it means a further options menu will open when rolled over.

Step 3
Open the folder and a whole range of further options are available along the top of the new window. You will see four main tabs along the top: File, Home, Share and View. Each one of these, when clicked, will display a different set of further options relevant to the section.

Step 4
Most of these options are self-explanatory, such as copy, paste and select all but some are a little more confusing. Most casual computer users won't need to use 90 per cent of the options in their day-to-day use but it is worth understanding them anyway. Add a few files to the folder and experiment.

Step 5
If you want to get really deep into managing your folders, there are even more options to explore. Open any folder and right-click anywhere inside the main window. From the action menu that appears, click Properties. Here you can manage all sort of things, from security to icon style.

Step 6
To change the icon style, that will change the style of all folder icons, click the customise tab and then click Change Icon at the bottom. Scroll to view all of the available icons (downloaded icons can be accessed by browsing), click on your preferred icon and click OK.

Using the Task View Feature

Windows 10 has made huge steps towards creating an operating system which is suited to everyone, including busy multitaskers. It's easier than ever to switch between tasks in Windows 10 and you can even have extra workspaces for when you're working in different apps. All these features are available inside a new Task View feature, available directly from a new taskbar icon.

Using Task View

Task View is a quick way to view and manage all of the windows and apps open on your PC at any given moment, even those that are minimised.

Step 1 There's an almost imperceptible new button on the Windows 10 taskbar next to the search box. It's the new Task View button and it gives you a new way to switch between apps. Microsoft has experimented with various task switchers over the last couple of versions of Windows and this is the latest iteration.

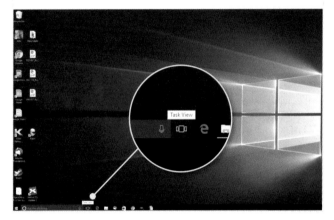

Step 2 Clicking the button (or pressing Windows + Tab) brings up this display. It's simple and remains active until you click on one of the apps to switch to that; or click on the taskbar, press Windows + Tab again or Esc to cancel. The more windows you have open, the smaller the thumbnails will be.

Step 3 As well as clicking on one of the apps you want to launch, you can also flick between them using the arrow keys and hit return on the one you want. What's more, you can also close apps from here too; as you hover over with the mouse, a cross will appear.

Step 4 If you're used to using Alt + Tab to flick between apps then don't worry, this feature is still enabled. However, as in previous versions of Windows, it's just for switching. Even though it looks like Task View, Alt + Tab just switches apps, it doesn't enable you to close them.

Using Virtual Desktops

The virtual desktop feature is a great way of separating apps, so you won't be distracted by your email while you're trying to get on with work.

Step 1 One of the great features in Task View is the ability to add extra desktops. Virtual desktops are essentially extra workspaces, so for example you can have one space with your email and chat windows open and another where you're working on a PowerPoint presentation without email distraction.

Step 2 Click or tap the Add a Desktop button at the bottom of the screen and you'll see an entirely blank desktop like this. Don't worry, you haven't just lost all the apps that were on your screen before, they're on the other desktop. Here we've opened two more apps in a completely different workspace.

Step 3 You can right-click the apps in Task View to send them to the other desktop, all clever stuff. At the bottom of the screen you'll see a representation of this desktop and your other desktop alongside it. If you hover over another desktop, you can see all the open apps on it.

Step 4 You can also drag apps between the open desktops by dropping them onto the appropriate desktop icon. An app can only reside on one desktop at once, so clicking an icon on the taskbar or Start menu could flip you between desktops if the app is open elsewhere.

Step 5 If you hover over the desktop icons, you'll see an X appear so you can close superfluous desktops down to save resources. Doing this doesn't close any apps down but it will add them to the oldest (original) desktop. They're called virtual desktops for a reason.

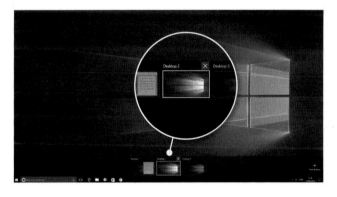

Step 6 Virtual desktops are great for having different areas for different tasks. However, if you wish you can select certain apps and have them appear on all open desktops. To do this, open Task View, right-click on an app and choose Show window on all desktops or Show windows from this app.

Using Windows 10 Snap Assist

One of the best features added in Windows 7 was Snap Assist, enabling you to 'snap' windows to the sides of the screen. With displays getting bigger, the logic is that we can have more windows on our screens. Being able to split the screen into different sections for different windows is useful and Snap Assist in Windows 10 is designed to help.

Snapping Windows

It is very easy to have several windows open after just a few minutes of working on your PC and it is equally easy to lose track of them. Snapping windows helps prevent that.

Step 1 To snap any open window or app to the side of the screen, left-click on the title bar at the top of it and drag it over to either the far left or right of the screen. Your mouse cursor will need to reach the edge, not just the side of the window, for this to work properly.

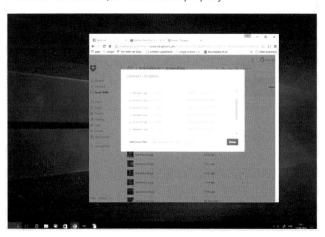

Step 2 As the cursor reaches the edge of the screen, a transparent outline will appear with a small flash, to show where the window will appear once snapped. Release the mouse button and the window will snap into place. You don't need to wait to see the outline, just drag and release.

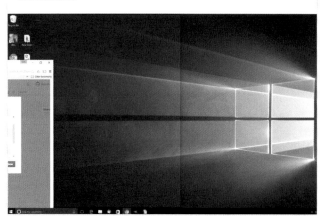

Step 3 If you have several windows open when you snap one to the left or right, the snap assist display will be shown. This display contains all of your other open windows as smaller thumbnails, positioned on the side of the screen opposite where you snapped the window.

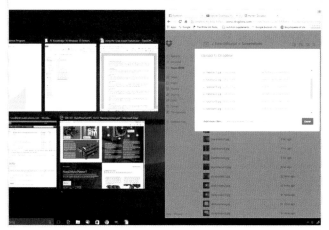

Step 4 Left-click on any of these thumbnails and that window will snap to the other side of the screen (opposite the one already snapped). You can also snap windows by selecting them and pressing the Windows key and an arrow button on your keyboard.

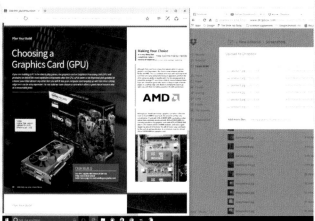

Step 5 You can also snap four windows in Windows 10, one into each corner of the screen. Having four windows snapped into the four corners of your screen is only really workable if you have a large monitor, although anyone with Windows 10 can do it.

Step 6 To snap four windows, you click and drag in the same way as explained above but you drag into the corners rather than just to the edge. You will see the transparent outline appear but it will now only cover a quarter of the screen. The snap assist display will still appear.

Step 7 You can also combine snapped windows in different ways. For example, one full height window snapped to the left, and two windows snapped in the two corners on the right, giving you three windows open at once but keeping one of the windows at a more usable size.

Step 8 To unsnap windows you simply click on the title bar of each window and drag it away from wherever it is snapped to: sides or corners. Snapping is a great multitasking tool and once you start using it, you won't want to go back to randomly floating windows.

Snapping Vertically

Windows 10 also adds support for vertical window snapping. This works slightly differently to normal windows snapping.

Step 1 Press Windows Key + Up or Windows Key + Down to snap the current app to the top or bottom halves of the screen. Pressing Windows Key + Up a second time will maximise the window, while pressing Windows Key + Down a second time will minimise it.

Step 2 You can't do this with the mouse, you need to use the keyboard shortcuts. Dragging a window's title bar to the top of your screen will just maximise it, while dragging it to the bottom of your screen won't do anything. Some universal apps may not behave well with vertical or 2×2 snapping.

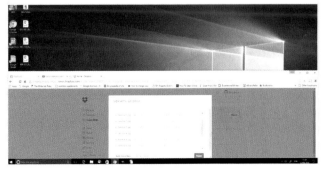

46 Essential Guide to Personalisation

Learn how to start making Windows 10 look and work perfectly just for you.

11:45
Wednesday, April 29

Team Dinner
Bento Box
6:00 PM – 12:00 PM

56 Install an Alternative Browser

Edge is a great browser but there is no reason why you can't choose another.

Firefox

Browse Freely

60 Manage Your Notifications

Easily learn to control how and when you are alerted to messages, emails and events.

Notifications

Show me tips about Windows
On

Show app notifications
On

Show notifications on the lock screen
On

Show alarms, reminders and incoming VOIP calls on the lock screen
On

Hide notifications while presenting
Off

Personalising Windows 10

Everything you need to start making Windows 10 work better for you is here! Learn how to make Windows 10 look and feel more personal to you, from changing the wallpaper, customising the Start menu and adding themes, to working with alternative browsers and controlling how the OS notifies you of those important messages and emails.

46 The Essential Guide to Personalisation

54 Using Sticky Notes in Windows 10

56 Installing Alternative Browsers

58 File Associations and Protocols

60 Managing Your Notifications

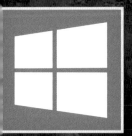

The Essential Guide to Personalisation

One of the most welcome features of Windows 10 is the return to the familiar desktop environment and there are many ways to customise it to suit your needs and tastes; including icon size, background image and colour scheme.

Change the Desktop Background

The Desktop personalisation procedure hasn't changed much since Windows 7, so if you've used that OS before this will feel very familiar.

Step 1 You can get started with personalising the Windows 10 Desktop in exactly the same way as you did with Windows 7. For anyone completely new to Windows, that means right-clicking anywhere on the Desktop screen and selecting Personalise from the action menu that appears.

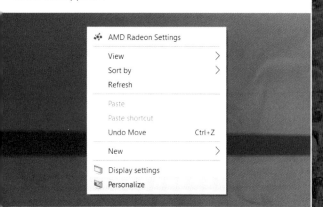

Step 2 The Background settings will be displayed first by default. Click the first drop-down menu to select whether to use the default backgrounds, solid colours or choose to display folders of your own images. Your choices here changes what is displayed in the background settings.

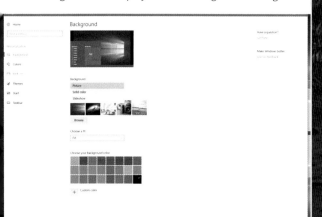

Step 3 To select your own pictures for the background, click on the Browse button and navigate to the folder containing the images you want to use. For best results, you might need to crop some of your pictures to the same aspect ratio, i.e. widescreen, as your monitor screen.

Step 4 To set a picture as your Desktop background, simply click on it. It will instantly be set as your new Desktop background image (a preview will display). The screen shows you the last five images used or you can click the Browse button to choose a new one from your folders.

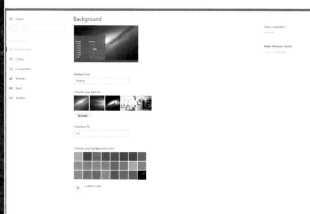

Step 5 If you opt for Slideshow, you will see some additional options to choose from. You can set the interval for the slide show from the 'Change picture every' menu and decide how you'd like the images to fit on the screen by clicking the 'Choose a fit' menu.

Step 6 Even if you set a background image, you can also change the colour of the actual desktop. Click on the Colours option at the bottom and choose a background colour. You can also choose a custom colour from a more detailed hexadecimal colour selector.

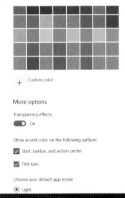

Set Accent Colours

By accent colours we mean the colour of the taskbar, the Start menu and the frames of new windows and so on, that you open on your computer.

Step 1 Apart from the desktop background, you can also change the colour of the taskbar and the Start menu and other system components. Click on the Colours option in the menu sidebar and choose an accent colour from the swatch. Recently selected colours are also displayed.

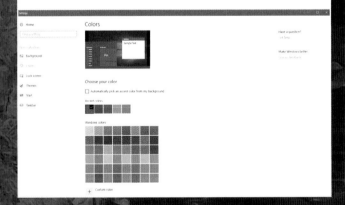

Step 2 You can also let Windows automatically match the accent colour to the current desktop image. This isn't a perfect solution and works best if the desktop background image you are using is predominantly one colour. To do this, just tick the checkbox.

Step 3 You can actually choose where the colour accent is applied. You can set it so it changes the Start, taskbar and Action Center and the Title bars of windows. You can also pick one or the other, or a combination of all options. You can also make these elements semi-transparent.

Step 4 Since the Creators update, most of the core Microsoft apps allow you to choose either a light or dark theme (several have had this option for a while now). You can set the default app theme colour in the colours section of personalisation; this can be overridden in the app settings.

Lock Screen Customisation

The lock screen can feature custom backgrounds with Spotlight Images, display app statuses, and even give you direct access to Cortana.

Step 1 The first thing to choose is whether to display one of your own images, a slideshow of images or something from Windows Spotlight. If you choose either of the first two of these, more options will appear to select the images you want to use (single or multiple).

Step 2 You will see that there are two separate sections for adding apps here. The section with the single app icon is the one which will display more detailed information and the section with seven icons/spaces for adding apps which will show quick statuses.

Step 3 You can add as many apps as you wish here, up to the maximum of eight. To choose which apps have statuses displayed, click on one of the spaces and choose from the pop-up menu that appears. The menu for the detailed information space will be slightly shorter than for quick statuses.

Step 4 You can check how the detailed and quick statuses are displayed on your lock screen by letting your PC sleep; or by pressing the Windows key and choosing Sleep. Be aware however, that statuses may not show up straight away for things like Messages and Email.

Step 5 There are several other lock screen customisation options here. You can choose whether to display an image on the sign-in screen as well as the main lock screen and there are direct links to Cortana settings, where you can control how Cortana works on the lock screen.

Step 6 The final two links take you to screen timeout and screen saver settings. The settings you choose there will depend on your personal preference and also on your computer location. Setting a shorter timeout means that your computer will be secure if you have to leave it.

Disable the Lock Screen

There is no setting to disable the lock screen completely but it is still possible to do by delving into the Registry. This is fairly advanced customisation, so approach with care.

Step 1 To access the Registry, press the Windows key + R, enter regedit, and then click OK. With the Registry open, navigate to HKEY_LOCAL_MACHINE\ SOFTWARE\Policies\Microsoft\Windows\. Right-click the final Windows folder and click New > Key.

Step 2 Name this new key "Personalisation" and then navigate inside it. Right-click inside the right-hand pane and select New > DWORD (32-bit) Value. Name it "NoLockScreen". Then double click this new value and change the Value data to 1. Then click OK and exit the Registry Editor.

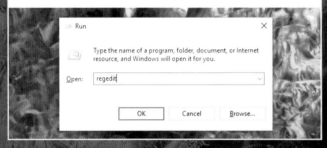

Adding New Themes

Themes can be added from a variety of sources but the best place to find them initially is the official theme page from Microsoft, or from the Windows 10 Store.

Step 1 You can access the current theme page in a couple of different ways. You can open the web browser and navigate to www.support.microsoft.com/en-gb/ themes, or Google "Windows 10 themes". Alternatively, open Settings > Personalisation > Themes and click 'Get more themes in the store'.

Step 3 Each theme is displayed with a thumbnail and the number of images supplied shown. The Microsoft theme page doesn't allow you to view all of these images before you download, you just have to base your choice on the title and thumbnail. Click Download on any you like the look of.

Step 2 All of these actions should bring you to the same themes page. Be aware that all themes here will soon be moved into the Windows Store app. Themes are listed in a variety of categories down the side of the page, ranging from Featured Themes, to themes with custom sounds supplied.

Step 4 Different themes will contain different amounts of content. Some might only have a colour profile and a few desktop wallpapers; others might contain icons, colours, wallpapers and sounds. Even the simplest of themes is likely to be more than just changing the desktop wallpaper.

Lock Screen Customisation

The lock screen can feature custom backgrounds with Spotlight Images, display app statuses, and even give you direct access to Cortana.

Step 1 Once a theme is downloaded, you may need to open it to activate it. You can do this directly from the download interface that appears at the bottom of the browser window (showing download progress) or you can go to your Downloads folder, right-click on the file and click Open.

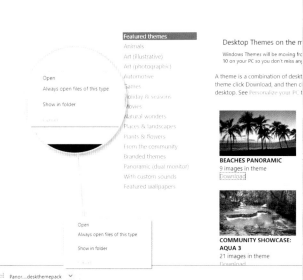

Step 3 Themes downloaded from the Windows Store won't need to be activated in this way. You can just click the Get button on the theme page in the store and then view the theme in settings > personalisation > themes. You can switch between themes here just by clicking the thumbnail.

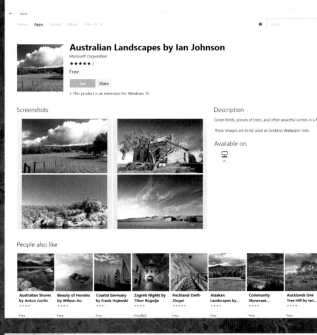

Step 2 The theme will then be applied, and the first desktop wallpaper in the sequence will appear on your screen. Any colour profile changes will also be applied. If you want to manage the theme settings, head to Settings > Personalisation > Themes > Theme Settings.

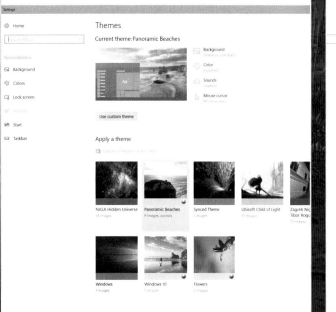

Step 4 Each theme applied can be customised further using the options in the Themes section. You can alter the background, colour, sounds and even the mouse cursor of any theme, making it completely unique to you. When you have chosen the changes, you will need to click Save Theme.

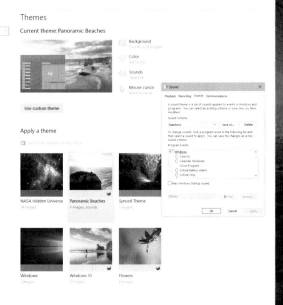

Change your Desktop icons

If you use desktop icons such as This PC, your personal folder or Network connections, you can change those icons. You can even download complete icon packs online, giving your desktop a completely different feel.

Step 1 Open the Personalisation screen of the Settings menu and select Themes from the sidebar menu. You now need to look for the Related Settings option. In the Related Settings section, click on the link to Desktop icon settings.

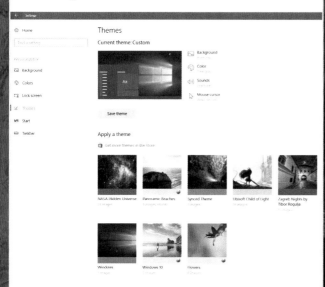

Step 3 If you wish to do so, it is possible to choose different icons for these system tools and you can even download custom icons online. To change the appearance of the desktop icons, click on the icon you want to change and then click the Change Icon button.

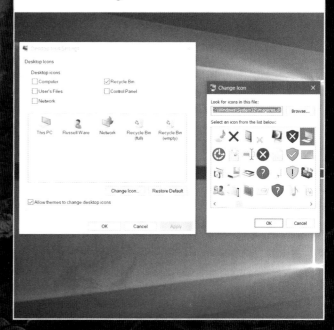

Step 2 The window that now opens lets you choose which default icons appear on your desktop. The Recycle Bin is just about essential but the others, including Computer, Users Files, Network and Control Panel icons are optional.

Step 4 The icon chooser window that appears will look very familiar to veteran Windows users, since it's essentially unchanged from Windows 98. Scroll through the gallery until you find an icon you like or use the Browse button to navigate to any icon pack you've downloaded.

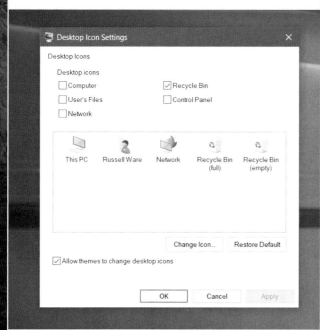

Personalise Windows Sounds

You don't like the default Windows sounds? You want to replace them with all your favourite Star Trek sound effects? No problem!

Step 1 To change the sounds that Windows uses to notify you about events and problems, open the Personalisation control panel as explained previously and click on Themes in the sidebar menu, then click on Advanced sound settings.

Step 2 To change a sound, first select it from the list of sounds shown in the Sounds control panel, then click on the Browse button. Navigate to the folder containing the sounds that you want to use and then double-click the new sound. You can click on the Test button to hear what it sounds like.

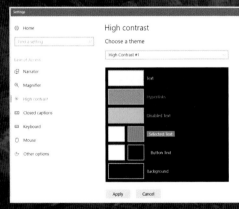

IMPROVING VISIBILITY

Windows 10 incorporates a number of features designed to improve accessibility for people with impaired sight, including a range of high contrast Desktop themes. You can activate these from the Personalisation control panel. Activate the panel by right-clicking on the Desktop and selecting Personalisation and then click on one of the high contrast themes presented. You can exit the theme by clicking back on the previous theme.

Personalise the Start Menu

The final Customisation menu option lets you customise the Start menu to a limited extent.

Step 1 You are presented with a list of toggle switches that activate certain options. The 'Use Start full screen' effectively returns you to the Windows 8.1 Start screen, so you'll probably want to leave it off unless you have a specific need for a full-screen menu.

Step 2 Clicking on 'Choose which folder appear on Start' lets you choose from a list of preinstalled shortcuts to your Library folders. Choose only those you really need to have there; otherwise the Start menu can quickly become hopelessly cluttered.

Add Tools to the Desktop

If you want to take your customisation of the desktop to the next level, you can begin to add desktop tools such as Rainmeter.

Step 1 Start by downloading the Rainmeter installer from the Rainmeter.net. To install the software, run the installer program that you downloaded and follow the instructions. You will have the choice to choose from the 32 or 64bit versions during the process.

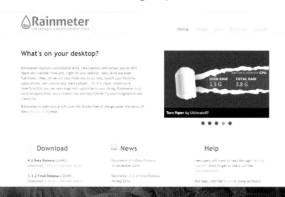

Step 2 The first time you run Rainmeter, your desktop will look something like the image here. Each small window on the right side of your screen (System, Disk, etc.) is a skin. This is the illustro skin set. The app remembers each skin's location and settings independently.

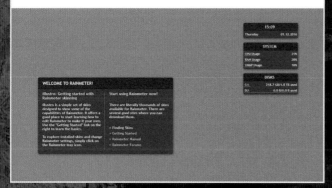

Step 3 To move a skin, just click and drag it to a new location. The easiest way to interact with Rainmeter skins is through the context menu (right-click on the skin). A skin may have any number of tabs, buttons, menus or other bells and whistles in its design.

Step 4 You can use the context menu to load skins from your library. Right-click on any of the skins and select illustro > Google > Google.ini. The Google skin will appear in the top left corner of your desktop. You can now drag it into place alongside your other skins.

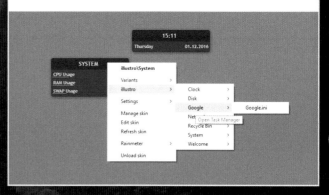

Step 5 You can also unload (remove) a skin with the context menu. Right-click the new Google skin and select Unload skin. You will see the skin fade away and disappear (useful for getting rid of the welcome skin). When a skin is unloaded, its location and settings are still saved.

Step 6 Skins can have different variations. To see an example of one with variants, right-click the Disk skin and select Variants in the context menu. Variants share the same location and settings, and only one of a skin's variants may be loaded at a time.

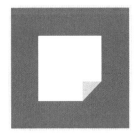

Using Sticky Notes in Windows 10

There are lots of Windows 10 apps for making to do lists and reminders but sometimes you just need a simple note to jog your memory when you boot up your PC. There is an often overlooked bit of software in Windows, available for some time now, that allows you to add sticky notes to your screen quickly and easily.

Adding Sticky Notes

The Sticky Notes software comes preinstalled with every version of Windows since Vista, although it has been improved slightly with each new release.

Step 1 You can find the Sticky Notes software in the All Apps menu of Windows 10 or you can search for "Sticky Notes" using the search field in the taskbar. If you can't find it under S in the main All Apps menu, it might be within the Windows Accessories folder instead. Click to open the first note.

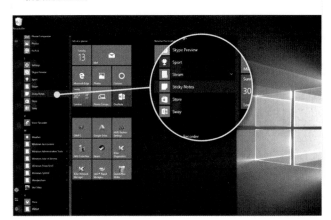

Step 2 A blank Sticky Note will now appear on your screen. You will see that it looks just like a real Post-it Note, except the corners won't curl up and the glue won't fail. Click anywhere on the body of the note to make the cursor appear, if it isn't visible to begin with.

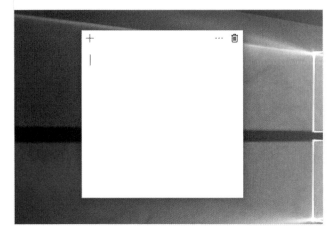

Step 3 You can now type out your note. This can be a simple "Remember to call Ian", a shopping list (with the formatting added yourself) or any other simple note you might need. The note is not confined to the size of the original sticky note, with a scroll handle appearing if you reach the bottom.

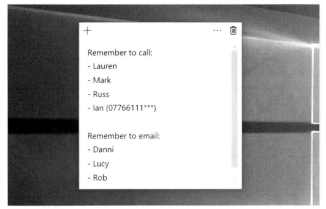

Step 4 You can resize the sticky notes, to make them slightly smaller or quite a bit larger, by moving the mouse pointer over the corner or edge until a handle icon appears and then clicking and dragging to the required size. This is useful if you don't want to scroll to see a longer note.

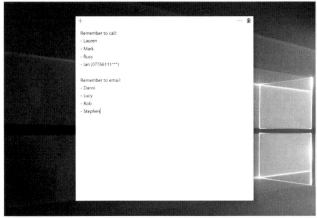

Step 5 Once you have created one note, adding another is easy. Click the + button in the top left and another yellow blank note will appear. Repeat until you have enough notes. You can also right click on the icon in the taskbar and then New Note or use the keyboard shortcut Ctrl + N.

Step 7 You don't have to stick to the default yellow colour note that you start with. Right click on any of your notes and then click the menu icon at the top and you can change the colour to a variety of presets. This is particularly handy if you want to make certain notes stand out.

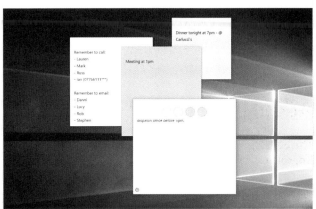

Step 6 You can move the notes around the desktop however you wish, even overlapping them if required. Your sticky notes will stay in the position you put them in, even when you shut down and restart your computer, as long as you don't close the software manually.

Step 8 You need to keep the app open for your notes to remain on the screen but as long as it is, you can shutdown and reboot and the notes will remain on the desktop. To close notes, you simply need to click on the trash icon in the top right corner. Close the last note and the software closes too.

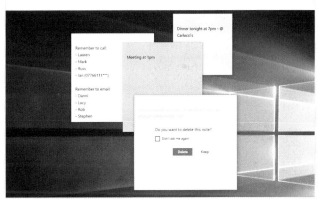

WINDOWS 10 ANNIVERSARY STICKY NOTES

Windows Ink, available for the first time in the Anniversary update, brings the writing you do every day into your digital world. Now, using a Windows 10 device, graphic designers can be more creative, musicians can write digital music, lawyers can edit documents with the power of the pen and students can make mathematical equations and learn by writing. All of this is available to any Windows 10 user, but even more useful for those with a touchscreen PC.

- Quickly and easily take a note, sketch on a screenshot or draw an idea.
- Smart Sticky Notes help you remember common tasks like reminding you of flight times or offering directions using Maps.
- Key apps have new Ink-specific features, like using handwriting in Office, Ink annotations in Microsoft Edge or drawing custom routes in Maps.

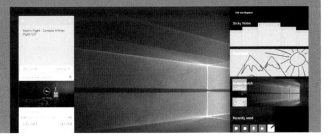

Installing Alternative Browsers

The Edge browser is a great tool for surfing the Internet but it isn't perfect and it certainly isn't as feature-rich as some of the more established web browsers available; but just because Edge comes preinstalled with Windows 10, that doesn't mean you can't install a second browser to use instead.

Browser Choice

There are dozens of different browsers available, from the market leaders such as Chrome and Firefox, to more specialised offerings which focus on security or speed.

Chrome Google Chrome is a freeware web browser developed by Google. It was first released in 2008 for Windows and was later ported to most other platforms. As of September 2016, StatCounter estimates that Chrome has a 62 per cent worldwide usage share of desktop web browsers.

Opera Opera is a web browser developed by Opera Software. The latest version is available for Microsoft Windows, macOS and Linux. Opera includes built-in tabbed browsing, a bookmarks bar, add-ons and a download manager. Opera Speed Dial allows users to add an unlimited number of pages shown in thumbnail form.

Firefox Firefox, or Mozilla Firefox, has consistently been one of the fastest browsers around since its launch more than 10 years ago. Features include tabbed browsing, spell checking, incremental find, live bookmarking, Smart Bookmarks, a download manager, private browsing and location aware browsing.

Torch If you really fancy something different, Torch is definitely niche. Torch is a Chromium-based web browser and Internet suite developed by Torch Media. Torch handles common Internet related tasks such as displaying media, sharing websites via social networks, accelerating downloads all directly from the browser.

Installing a Browser

Installing an alternative browser is very easy once you have decided which one to go for. Let's take a quick look at the process of installing Google Chrome.

Step 1 To install Chrome for your user account, the first thing you need to do is download the installer file from https://www.google.com/chrome/browser/desktop/index.html. Just click the big blue button and wait for the installation to finish.

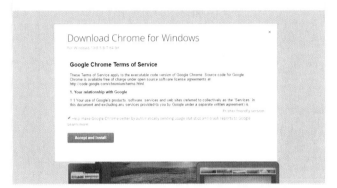

Step 2 When prompted at the bottom of the browser windows (where download progress is shown), click Run or Save. If you chose Save, double-click the installer file to start the installation process. Follow the steps shown on screen to complete this part of the process.

Step 3 If you have used Chrome in the past, on a previous PC or before you installed Windows 10, you should have a Google account. Use this to sign in and Chrome will import all of your previous bookmarks, settings and extensions. Click Settings > Sign in to Chrome.

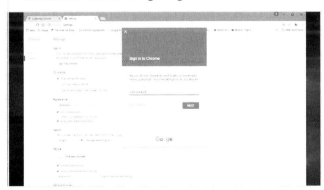

Step 4 Signing in to Chrome connects your Google Account to your browser for a more personalised browsing experience. All your Chrome data, like your bookmarks, history, passwords and other settings, is synced to your Google Account and available on any device where you sign in to Chrome.

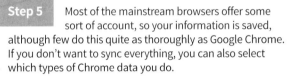

Step 5 Most of the mainstream browsers offer some sort of account, so your information is saved, although few do this quite as thoroughly as Google Chrome. If you don't want to sync everything, you can also select which types of Chrome data you do.

Step 6 You can customise Google Chrome to open any page for the homepage or start-up page. Your start-up page is the one that shows when you first launch Chrome on your computer. Your homepage is the one you go to when you click Home. Head into Settings and look for the relevant section.

File Associations and Protocols

Windows 10 comes with its own default set of associations that open specific file types. A file association controls which apps or programs are set to open which types of files. If you're not happy with the default associations and want to choose your own, it's easy to do.

Default Programs and Protocols

The ability to change the default apps and programs that Windows 10 uses goes a long way to helping you take full control of your PC and the system software.

Step 1 Click on the search bar on the left of the taskbar and type "default programs". You can also navigate to this settings tool by opening the All Apps list, scrolling down to W and clicking Windows System > Default Programs. Either way, open the tool on screen.

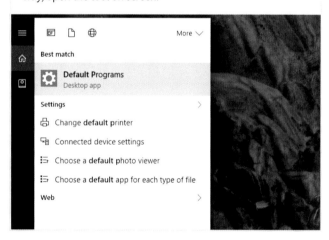

Step 2 A list of apps already associated with various functions will appear. Click on any of these to see alternative options. The options shown will vary depending on the apps you have installed at this time. If a function has no apps associated with it, you can click 'Look for app in the Store'.

Step 3 Below the description, you will see two options: Set this program as default and Choose defaults for this program. The amount of default file associations is also shown. Click 'Set this program as default' first.

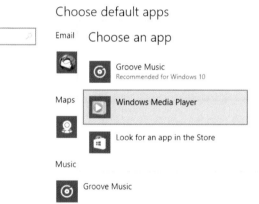

Step 4 Next, click on the 'Choose default apps by file type' option to see a list of all the file types that can be associated with your currently installed apps. These are the types of files which will automatically open in that app when clicked. Anywhere a + is shown, is without a default app.

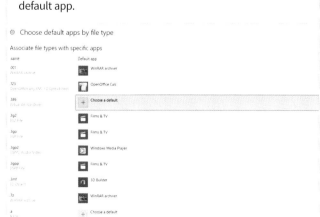

Step 5 You can also choose default apps based on protocols. This generally means that typing or accessing a certain URL will trigger the app to open, rather than a webpage. For example, if MAILTO is detected by the browser, our default email client (Thunderbird) will launch to handle the request.

Step 6 Finally, you have the ability to set defaults by app, rather than choosing apps to go with certain files or actions. Click 'Set defaults by app' at the bottom of the screen. A new window will open, displaying a list of apps on the left. Click on any app you want to change the defaults for.

Step 7 You now have two options: Setting the app as default for any and all files or protocols it can open, or choosing individual defaults the app will use. Clicking the first results in an instant change, clicking the second will show you a list of current defaults for that app, allowing you to choose.

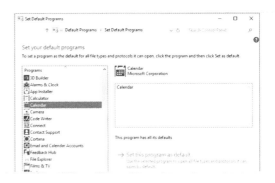

Step 8 If you run into problems after changing protocols and defaults, you can easily reset to the Microsoft recommended defaults with a click of the button on the Default Programs screen. This may mean that you have to go back through your list and change some settings but it can be a useful fix.

Running Services

Being able to check which Windows Services are running at any particular time is also a useful option, as it can help to diagnose performance or stability issues

Step 1 The easiest way to get to the Services panel is by going through the Power User menu. Right-click on the Start menu button on the far left of the taskbar and select 'Computer Management' from the menu that pops up; this is the Power User or Win-X menu.

Step 2 Click the 'Services and Applications' option in the left-hand panel of the window that opens. Then click 'Services' to show the full list. The list will be large but not all services will be running at any one time. Click on any to see more details, including management option, for that service.

Managing Your Notifications

If you've used a modern smartphone, you'll be all too familiar with Notifications, those urgent little messages that tell you something has just happened. Windows 10 seems to have embraced notifications in a much bigger way than older versions. This is how to manage those popups.

It's a feature of modern life in the digital age that we don't have to remember things anymore. Just a decade or so ago we used to have to remember dozens of phone numbers but with mobile phones now storing all our contacts we're lucky if we can remember our own number. We used to have to remember facts but today we have Wikipedia constantly at our fingertips. We used to have to remember appointments and tie a knot in a hanky to remember to buy a pint of milk but these days we have Notifications to remind us of everything. These changes in the ways that we find and use knowledge is actually changing the ways that our brains work; as we rely more on machines to store and recall everyday information, our memories are becoming less efficient, although our critical faculties may be improving to help us weed out false information. Whether this is a good thing or not, only time will tell.

Notifications have become an everyday fact of life for anyone who uses a smartphone, tablet or personal computer. All through the day you'll hear that insistent little "ping" that lets you know that

you've received an email, or one of your friends has posted another cat picture on Facebook and that you've only got 15 minutes to get to the dentist. While they can certainly be useful for anyone trying to juggle a job, family and busy social life, if you don't manage your notifications you'll never get a moment's peace. The same is true of Windows Notifications; if you don't set them up properly you'll be constantly notified about things that you just don't need to know about.

First introduced with Windows 8, Notifications are the messages that pop up in the bottom right-hand corner of your screen, reminding you of calendar events, letting you know that you've got emails and generally keeping you informed about what's going on with your life and your computer. There's no doubt that Notifications are useful, especially when they remind you of a forgotten appointment or signal the arrival of an important email. However if you don't take a firm hand with them you can be overwhelmed with pop-up messages about trivial Twitter posts or friends' Facebook status updates.

Notification Settings

In Windows 10 you can choose what sort of Notifications you receive and even decide which apps can post Notifications and what type of Notifications each app can use. Read on to find out how you can manage your notifications.

Step 1 To view your recent Notifications, click on the Action Center icon in the System Tray area of the Task Bar, at the bottom right of the screen. It's the one that looks like a rectangular speech bubble.

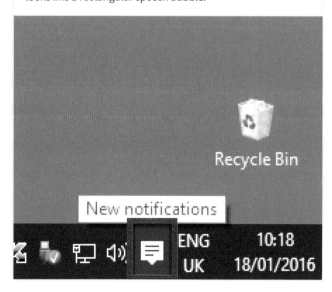

Step 2 The Action Center sidebar will open, showing all your recent Notifications, as well as a panel of buttons at the bottom of the screen. Click on All Settings to open the Settings screen.

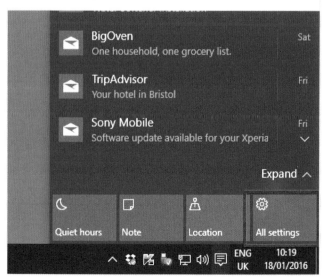

Step 3 Here's our disk usage – as you can see it's pretty active! You will also have this if you have several big apps open (we've got Edge, Spotify, Word and Excel open in this example). In the previous step you could see our processor usage, and as you may have noticed, we've only been using around 40 per cent of its capability during the last minute.

← Settings

⚙ SYSTEM

Display
Notifications & actions
Apps & features
Multi-tasking
Tablet mode
Power & sleep
Storage
Offline maps
Default apps

Quick actions

Choose your quick actions

[🌙] [📝] [📍] [⚙]

Select which icons appear on the taskbar

Turn system icons on or off

Notifications

Show me tips about Windows
[●○] Off

Show app notifications

Step 4 Wi-Fi usage (you can also see wired network usage if you use that to connect) is more sporadic as the network connection tends to be used intermittently – unless you're copying files or similar. Here we're streaming music, which appears to download in chunks. Notice there's no data being received or sent right at this moment.

Notifications

Show me tips about Windows
[○●] On

Show app notifications
[○●] On

Show notifications on the lock screen
[○●] On

Show alarms, reminders and incoming VOIP calls on the lock screen
[○●] On

Hide notifications while presenting
[●○] Off

Step 5 The Start-up tab is one of the most important in Task Manager. While you can configure an app such as Skype to start-up when Windows does and disable the same within the app, some applications are sneaky and enable themselves to start when Windows does. Here you can select the app and either enable or stop this from happening.

Notifications

Show me tips about Windows
[●○] Off

Show app notifications
[●○] Off

Show notifications on the lock screen
[○●] On

Show alarms, reminders and incoming VOIP calls on the lock screen
[○●] On

Step 6 Although it's of limited general use, the Users tab details what apps and processes are running on a per-user basis. This might be useful if your PC is running slowly and you want to see what resources someone else who is logged into the PC is hogging. They might have something wasteful running in the background, for example.

Show notifications from these apps

AAM Updates Notifier Application
Off   [●○] Off

AcroTray
Off   [●○] Off

Adobe Reader and Acrobat Manager
Off   [●○] Off

Calendar
On: Banners, Sounds   [○●] On

Dropbox
On: Banners   [○●] On

Facebook
On: Banners   [○●] On

Google Drive
On: Banners   [○●] On

Step 7 The Details tab is really for pro users only and has full information on each running process and which user is responsible for it. You can also see how much resource the process is taking up as well as what is called a Process ID, or PID, that identifies the process on your machine.

Calendar
On: Banners, Sounds   [○●] On

Dropbox
Off   [●○] Off

Facebook
Off   [●○] Off

Google Drive
Off   [●○] Off

Mail
On: Banners   [○●] On

News
On: Banners, Sounds   [○●] On

Step 8 Services are programs that run in the background. The chances are your PC is running lots of them. For example Windows Defender, the built-in security software, runs in the background as a service. As well as viewing the active services in Task Manager, you can click the Open Services link to manage services on your PC.

← Settings

⚙ FACEBOOK

Notifications
[○●] On

Show notification banners
[○●] On

Play a sound when a notification arrives
[●○] Off

Getting Online

68 How to Use Microsoft Edge

Learn all the tips and tricks you need to use the new Edge browser.

74 Using the Cortana Assistant

Find out exactly what the Cortana assistant can do for you, day-to-day.

80 How to Set Up Your Email

Discover ways to make sending, receiving and managing your emails easier.

Getting Online with Windows 10

Although they might seem like simple tasks, browsing the web, sending and receiving emails and searching off and online successfully are some of the core skills any Windows 10 user should be comfortable with. The guides in this section will help that happen, but will also take your knowledge to the next level.

64   Connecting to the Internet

66   Exploring the Edge Browser

68   Using the Edge Browser

72   Searching with Windows 10

74   Using the Cortana Assistant

78   Exploring the Windows 10 Mail App

80   Set Up and Use Email and Accounts

Connecting to the Internet

Setting up your Internet connection, also known as a network, is an important step in learning Windows 10. Joining and managing networks in Windows 10 is easier than ever. One of the new features is Wi-Fi Sense that enables you to securely share network connection details with your contacts, so you can connect to networks that are trusted by your friends without any effort.

Manage Your Network Settings

We'll show you how to master your Wi-Fi settings and explain what you need to do if you have a problem connecting to the Internet in Windows 10.

Your Settings Network and Internet is one of the key sections within the new Windows 10 Settings app. It features a plethora of settings for the different ways to connect to the Internet. While the Wi-Fi screen is fairly straightforward, there are different settings windows for Ethernet connections and even dial-up.

VPN Settings If you need to log into a corporate network, this is where you need to enter the appropriate settings. It's fairly easy to do but you'll need the configuration details from your IT helpdesk (they will have to enable you to have VPN access) plus your username and password.

Wi-Fi Sense We don't mind ourselves but some people are worried about the security implications of sharing network settings; or simply don't want to automatically connect to networks shared by others. You can disable it by visiting the right settings; just click Manage Wi-Fi Settings from the Wi-Fi window. You can also manage your known networks here.

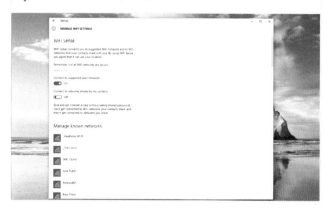

Proxy Settings If you use a proxy server, this is where you enter any specific settings to do with that. However, Windows 10 should automatically detect proxy settings. Note that the settings you configure here won't apply if you connect via a VPN, because a VPN is essentially a tunnel directly into the corporate network you're connecting to.

Your Usage

In a move designed to keep up with more mobile-based computing devices like the iPad, Windows 10 now includes a data usage page in Settings too. Here it splits your data between wired and wireless. We'd like to see more advanced settings than this too, so you could see how much data you used on a public wireless hotspot, for example.

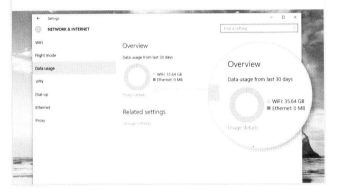

Troubleshoot

From the Network and Sharing Center you can also click the Troubleshoot Problems button if you're having issues with connectivity and networking. Another way to troubleshoot problems with a Wi-Fi connection is to right-click the Wi-Fi icon in your Notifications area near the clock. Select Troubleshoot Problems from the menu that appears.

Control Panel

Here we've left the Settings app and we're now in the Network and Sharing Center within Control Panel. The easiest way to get to this is to search for it or go to the Control Panel by right-clicking the Start button and selecting it from the menu. You can also get to it by right-clicking any network icon in the notifications area near the clock.

Disable Adapters

Another thing you can do is to disable and re-enable your network adapter (like the Wi-Fi card in your laptop). View your network connections by clicking Change Adapter Settings in the Network and Sharing Center and then right-clicking the network connection in question in the view above. Disable it and then re-enable.

Sharing Settings

From the previous window, select Change Advanced Sharing Settings from the left-hand sidebar. You'll be taken to this screen where you can turn on network discovery; this governs whether your computer can see others on your network and whether you are visible to them. You can also turn file and printer sharing on or off.

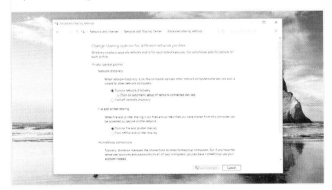

Firewall

Another thing to bear in mind is the Windows Firewall. Normally you won't have any dealings with this whatsoever but if you're having problems accessing the Internet with a particular app, ensure it is listed here. Go to Control Panel > Update and Security > Windows Firewall and then select Allow an App or Feature through Windows Firewall.

Exploring the Edge Browser

Microsoft Edge lets you move quickly from browsing to doing. Write or type notes dircctly on web pages and share them with others, read online articles free of distraction and save your favourite reads for convenient access later.

Browser Controls

Up in the top left corner, where you would probably expect to find them, are the browser controls. These include the button to add a new tab, the page refresh button and the page forward/page back buttons. Right-click on the main tab and you will see additional options, including Re-open Closed Tab.

Search Bar

There's no need to go to a website to search for pictures of adorable penguins or cute kittens. Stay put and save time by entering your search in the handy address bar. You'll get search suggestions, instant results from the web and your browsing history on the spot.

News Feed

The main home screen of Microsoft Edge is your News Feed. The news feed is provided by MSN and is made up of news stories based on your geographical location. If you are in the UK, the news will be from UK news websites, in the US, the news will be from American sources.

Task View

The taskbar, which remains at the bottom of the screen when using Edge, contains a button that switches to Task View. Task View allows you to quickly view any open windows and folders, displaying them as thumbnails. This includes any open Edge browser windows.

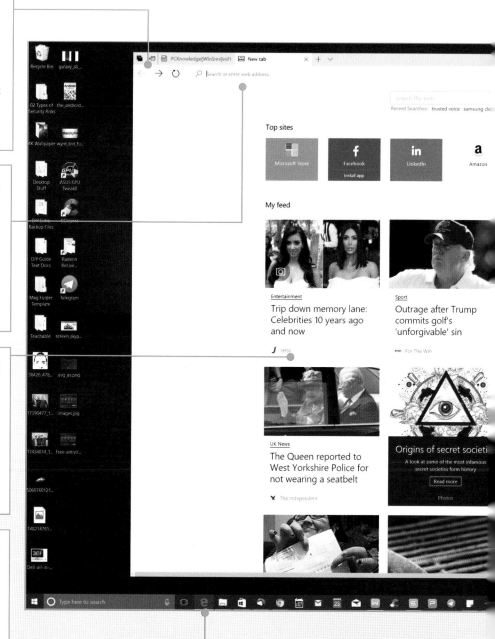

EDGE SETTINGS

Alongside options to change the style of the Edge browser, including changing to a dark theme, are several important settings. You can choose how the Edge browser opens, showing the Start page or another specified page for example. The advanced settings include options to block pop-ups and allow Flash Player.

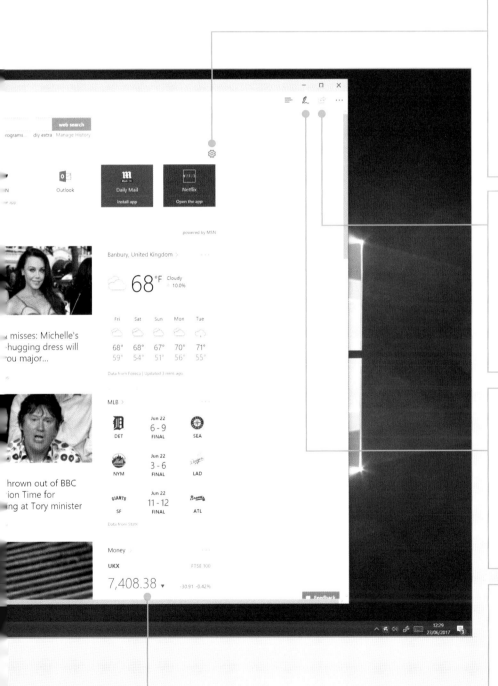

Customise Feed

You can customise the news feed to provide stories and articles that interest you personally. Click the "Customise" button and then choose your required location (UK, US, etc.). You can then click on the various categories, including: Entertainment, Money and Sport, and make them your favourites.

Share

Windows Edge gives you more ways to share your discovered content than ever before. Click the Share button whilst on any web page and the Sharing panel will open. The title of the page will be displayed. Click this to choose whether to share a link or a screenshot. Then click the app you wish to share with.

Web Note

Microsoft Edge on Windows 10 allows you to hand write notes on top of ANY website you visit. When you are on a website and want to add a written note, simply click the Web Note button. A new menu bar opens, allowing you to choose pen colour and thickness. Now write your note and click Save.

The Hub

The taskbar contains shortcuts to many of the most commonly used apps, including: the Edge browser, the App Store and File Explorer. You can add any app to the taskbar by right-clicking on the tile or app icon and selecting "Pin to Taskbar" from the menu.

Using the Edge Browser

Microsoft Edge replaces the old and creaky Internet Explorer as the main preinstalled Internet access tool in Windows 10. Edge is focused on modern web standards and is designed to be safe and fast. It also boasts several innovative features, such as the ability to highlight parts of web pages and share them with others.

Get Started with Edge

Edge is fast and fluid and we think you'll like it. It may not have the capability of Chrome or Firefox as yet but for basic web browsing it's almost perfect.

Step 1 Microsoft Edge carries on Internet Explorer's use of a stylised 'e' as its logo. This is to make things simple for users who are familiar with Internet Explorer. Click on this icon in the taskbar to open Edge or on the Start menu and find it in the All Apps list.

Step 2 If you're familiar with almost any modern browser, you will instantly be at home. The forward, back and refresh panel is almost identical to other browsers. The default new tab page shows your most visited sites but you can have news from MSN appear instead.

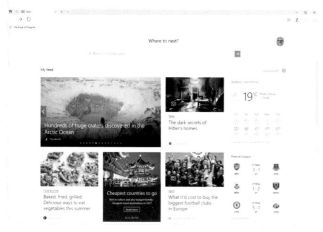

Step 3 As well as Edge's main controls in the top left, there are other items in the top right including the main menu to access more options. This is shown by the ellipsis (…) icon. From the main menu you can open a new window or a new InPrivate window as well as zoom into the current page.

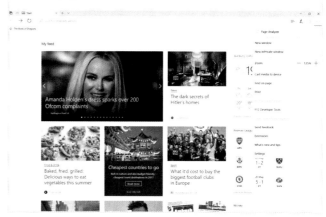

Step 4 You can begin using Edge by typing a search term or a complete website URL (address) in the search field near the top of the screen. Search results are then displayed in a fairly standard mixed list of links, images and videos. Click on any of them to see the website they link to.

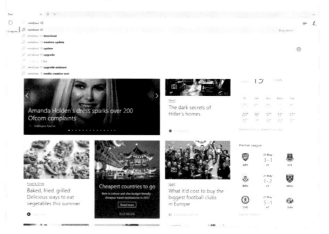

Customising Microsoft Edge

Once you become accustomed with the basics of Microsoft Edge you can start to explore the many options and settings available for personalising and customising.

Accessing the Settings

From this menu you're also able to access Settings as well as Print and Find, to locate a word or phrase in the open web page. Another option enables you to pin a particular web page to the Start menu as a tile should you wish to.

Change the Search Engine

Microsoft Edge is set to use Bing as its default search engine but you can change search provider in the Advanced Settings menu. As you type into Edge's search box, the browser recommends search suggestions. You can turn this off here should you want to. We find it quite useful.

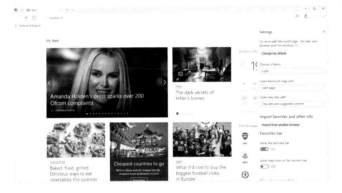

Advanced Edge Settings

The basic Settings menu is pretty lean on options but an Advanced Settings button at the bottom takes you into another menu with further options. This part of Edge is for more advanced users and it covers privacy, such as enabling browser cookies and other security settings.

The Edge Sidebar

Again in the top right, the ≡ icon launches the sidebar featuring your Reading List, Favourites, Downloads and History. If you've used Internet Explorer at all recently, this sidebar will be familiar to you as it's basically the same interface element. However, Reading List is new.

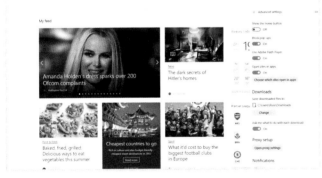

Change the Edge Theme

As well as the 'light' default theme of Microsoft Edge, there's an option in Settings to display a black theme. It's becoming a lot more common for applications to have dark themes, with the Windows 10 taskbar dark too. It's a good alternative to having super bright apps.

Pinning the Sidebar

In the top right of the sidebar there's a pin to keep the sidebar open, rather than just temporarily. You can move easily between your Reading List, Favourites, Downloads and History; just use the icons at the top of the bar to select the one you need.

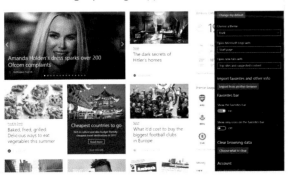

Microsoft Edge

Set Aside Tabs

You can now set tabs aside, rather than closing them completely, so that they are easier to go back to later. Tabs that are set aside should not take up bandwidth, so you don't need to worry about lots of open tabs slowing down your browsing. Tabs set aside are still there even after closing Edge.

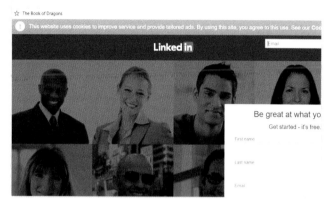

View and Restore Tabs

Tabs that are set aside can be viewed in the new Tab Viewer. You can access this by clicking the small down-facing arrow next to the New Tab button at the top of the window. Clicking any tab here switches to it. Alternatively, click the Tabs sidebar button at the top left of the window.

Import Your Bookmarks

Edge now makes it easy to import bookmarks saved in another browser (Google Chrome for example). Quickly get your bookmarks, saved passwords and browsing history from other places on your PC by selecting More > Settings > Import from another browser, and then choosing the correct one.

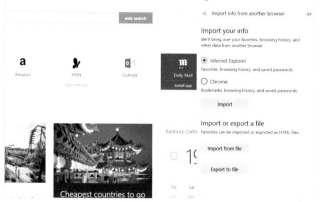

Read eBooks in Edge

The latest update to Microsoft Edge lets you read eBooks in .epub format. Books in this format automatically open in Edge when double-clicked. They can then be saved to the Reading List for easier viewing at a later date. Take a look at www.feedbooks.com/publicdomain for some freebies.

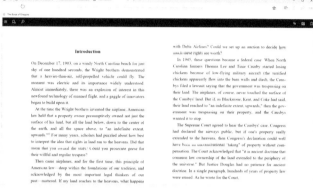

Enable the Favourites Bar

One of the folders is called Favourites Bar. This is a bar you can toggle on and off to permanently display certain Favourites in a strip underneath the address bar. To enable this feature, go to Settings via the main menu and switch the Favourites bar on using the toggle.

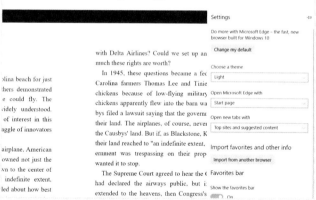

Annotating Pages

Making notes on web pages and sharing the results is one of the best new features in Edge. Launch this mode using the pen button next to the sidebar control in the top right of the main window. The editing controls include a pen, a highlighter, an erase function, an annotation feature and a copy tool.

Microsoft Edge Extensions

A new addition to the Edge browser in the Windows 10 Anniversary update is extensions. Extensions are small pieces of software you can add to Edge to give additional functions.

Step 1   Open the Edge browser on your PC and look for the small menu button at the top right of the window. Click this and then click the new Extensions link. When the extensions panel opens for the first time, it should be empty apart from a link to Get extensions from the Store.

Step 2   Click the link and the Microsoft Store app opens, displaying the available extensions. There are not that many to choose from right now but more will be added as app developers learn to take advantage of this new Anniversary feature in Windows 10.

Step 3   Click on any of the extension icons shown to open the information page. This tells you more about what the extension does, which devices it is available on and the minimum system requirements to run it properly. Scroll down the page to see user reviews and recommended extensions.

Step 4   To begin installation of your chosen extension, click the Get button at the top of the page. This then changes to show installation progress which, depending on the size of the extension, should take just a few seconds. The button then changes to say Launch.

Step 5   Clicking Launch will take you back to Edge with the extensions sidebar open. You then need to choose to enable the extension in Edge or keep it turned off for the present. Important information, such as whether the extension needs access to certain details on your PC is shown.

Step 6   How you use your new extension depends on what it actually does. The one we installed here is for analysing the structure of websites, so when we get to a website we want to examine, we have to click the menu button and then select the extension from the list at the top.

Searching with Windows 10

Until you use it, it's difficult to put into words just how much better Search is in Windows 10 than in previous versions of Windows. Microsoft did have a lot of ground to make up to match the search functions on offer in rival operating systems such as Apple's macOS.

Find Whatever You Want

Search now not only finds files, but settings, emails and apps too. You can even search for websites as well, providing you're happy with results from Microsoft's own Bing search engine. Here's how to make Search work for you.

Improved Search If you need to search for anything on your Windows 10 PC, the taskbar search bar is now the place to do it. You can still hit the Start button (or Start key on your keyboard) and start typing if you used to do that to search in previous versions of Windows.

Browser Search Launching a web search via the taskbar search will use your default browser, so if you have Google Chrome installed, you can launch that. But at the moment it will use Bing to perform the search rather than Google – this may change in due course.

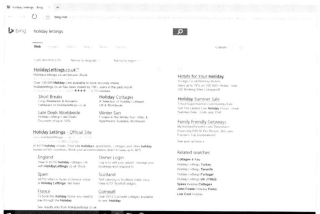

Search the Web As well as files and folders, you can also launch a web search from the taskbar. Note that you can filter the search menu by 'My Stuff' or 'Web', although we haven't filtered this view. Note the file name at the top is the closest match, rather than being an exact match.

Apps and Settings As well as files and folders, Windows 10 search can be used to find settings (such as the Power Options shown here) or apps (such as PowerPoint in this example). Hitting return will launch the top result, while you can always click on the result you want, of course.

Search Settings

Incorporating web searches in Windows 10's taskbar search may not be everyone's cup of tea, so you can turn this off should you wish – just hit the cog in the left-hand sidebar to go to Settings and turn this off. We find it useful a lot of the time, however.

What is Cortana?

Another setting you can change is to turn on Cortana. This is Microsoft's virtual assistant. Essentially this means that you can ask natural questions in the search bar – such as 'what will the weather be like in Doncaster today?' as well as give it voice commands. We've covered Cortana in a lot more detail overleaf.

Diverse Results

Don't be surprised to see very diverse results turn up in Windows 10's search. If you type something generic (such as 'man' in this example) you'll get results in apps, files, folders and settings simply because that kind of phrase is used as part of other words and, therefore, names of things in Windows.

My Stuff

If you do select to search 'My Stuff' only using the option at the bottom of the search results pop-up, this is the kind of thing you'll see. As you can see we've used another generic phrase for effect – 'pod' – which has found podcasts and some images of old iPod accessories. You're able to refine the search using the drop-down.

In-app Search

Search has also been improved within apps. Like in Windows 8.1, most apps have a search box in the top right. If you used Windows 8 you'll remember that searching was down via the Charm bar (swiping in from the right) and it would adjust to search within whatever app you were in. This has gone for good.

File Explorer Search

You can always search for files and folders in File Explorer as you could in previous versions of Windows. With the new taskbar search you won't need to use this as often as you did, but it's still there if you need it. We don't find it as quick as the taskbar search, though.

Using the Cortana Assistant

Cortana is Microsoft's 'virtual assistant'. If you've heard of Siri on the iPhone, it's very similar. You can talk to it, while it will pick out relevant information that's appropriate for you. If that sounds like it's too much, we'd encourage you to give it a chance.

Meet Your Digital Assistant

The Cortana personal assistant could well be a completely new experience for many users. So we've gone into quite a lot of detail here in order to give you the complete picture on how Cortana can be of help to you day-to-day.

Welcome to Cortana On the previous pages we talked you through Search in Windows 10. Cortana is like a layer on top of this search; you can either enable it or ignore it. Cortana isn't on by default in Windows 10. To enable it, click the Circle icon at the bottom of the Search sidebar.

Tell it Your Name Now you'll begin a bit of further personalisation of Cortana so it understands your voice and, as here, knows your name. As the Microsoft statement said in the previous step, you can always change individual parts of what Cortana remembers (via the Notebook, which we'll come onto shortly) or disable it entirely.

Setting Up Click Next and you'll see this screen. Basically, you'll need to allow Cortana to access all the information on the rest of your computer. It sounds alarming that you're enabling Cortana to look at your Calendar, browsing history and so on, but it needs to process this information to make things relevant for you.

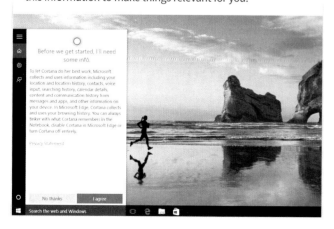

Allow Location Access As with virtual assistants on mobiles, Cortana works best when it knows where you are in the world. All our phones know where we are, so why not your PC? Unless you've a specific reason to forbid it, we recommend letting Cortana know your location.

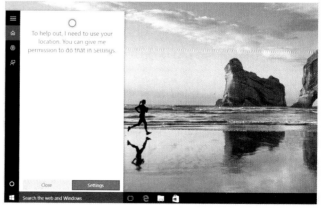

Location Settings

If you're concerned about the amount of location access you're giving at any time, you can always disable Location completely in the Settings app. You're also able to decide what apps have access. If you want to turn it off temporarily, you can do this using the Location button at the bottom of the Action Center.

Set Up Your Microphone

If you want to talk to Cortana (or at least have the option to), you'll need to ensure it can hear you correctly. Here we've got a problem with our microphone which we need to remedy. Many desktop PCs won't have microphones unless you have one in your webcam or another accessory, for example.

Get in Training

As with any app that requires talking to your PC, Cortana will take you through a little bit of training. It will adjust to your voice and the distance you are from your microphone. Some laptop microphones are especially bad, so Windows needs to compensate for that.

Back to Cortana

We've trained, we've configured and we've allowed Cortana full access. Let's see what Cortana has for us… Don't forget you can still use the search bar just as before. Cortana is another way to search, providing different information. It doesn't have to be seen as a replacement.

Your Interests

To finish the setup, Cortana will pick you a few starter interests. This changes the default content you'll see when you click the search box to bring up Cortana. Now, it's perfectly possible Cortana could pick you the wrong stuff. It's all part of the process as, if you correct it, Cortana will learn from its mistakes.

Changing Settings

So Cortana picked us out a batch of things including general news. To change these further, bring up the Cortana menu from the left-hand sidebar and bring up Notebook. Note that Reminders is a further useful feature; you can ask Cortana to remind you to go shopping at 12 or home at 5, it's completely up to you.

Your Notebook

As you can see, your Notebook (we don't think it's a particularly accurate name) contains various interests that Cortana will show you information about, as well as access to Cortana's settings (more on those shortly) and your personal information. Connected Accounts will show other things Cortana is connected to, like Microsoft Office.

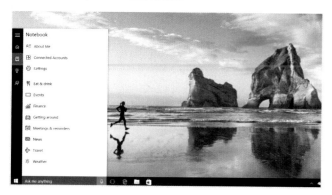

Change an Interest

If you want to disable or enable an interest for Cortana, click that particular option. You'll then see a window like this one, which enables us to enable or disable the interest as well as fine-tune the details. In this case, we can select which stocks and shares we'd like Cortana to show us.

The Main Cortana View

So we've gone back to the main Cortana window, where we're shown some automated content we'll talk you through in a second. Once again, if you start typing or say something if you've got voice set up, this automated content will disappear in favour of the Search menu.

Popular Now

If you scroll down the Cortana window there are other things for you to browse through, most of it powered by Bing, Microsoft's web portal, which gathers news and entertainment from various sources. There's an area for articles that are popular now and you can click through to anything that's of interest.

Eat and Drink

If you selected the oddly-named Eat and Drink as an interest, you'll see restaurant settings from Yelp or Foursquare. In the settings you can say how often you like to go out, what your budget is and how far you usually like to go. Most useful for regular business travellers, we'd have thought.

Weather

Probably Cortana's most used feature is that it will present you with weather for your current location. Clicking on it for more information will launch the Windows 10 Weather app (which is rather good, so no problems there), although the basic forecast should be enough for most needs.

'Hey Cortana'

In Settings, you can turn Cortana off completely as well as choose whether it should present you with flight and other transportation information. To track this Cortana will read your emails! There's also the option here to have your device constantly listening out for Cortana requests beginning with 'Hey Cortana'.

Speaking to Cortana

So if you enable it, saying 'Hey Cortana' will wake up Cortana. You'll see the search box jump into life and you can then launch into your question pretty much straight away. Alternatively, you can just click the microphone icon on the right-hand end of the search bar.

Asking Natural Questions

The idea is that you should be able to ask Cortana quite natural questions. Here we've asked what the weather will be like at the weekend, but you could equally ask if you'll need your umbrella. You can also ask specifics like "where is good round here for Italian food?".

Find a Setting

Of course, asking natural questions also means you can ask about where things are on your PC. Here we've asked where we can find the settings for Windows 10's Tablet mode, which are now opening. Clever stuff. If you're willing to talk to your PC, you can really speed things up.

Find an App

And here we're finding an app – the oft used Calculator which receives a bit of a makeover in Windows 10. By the way, it will use more laptop or tablet battery life if you do enable the setting that enables you to say 'Hey Cortana' to wake up the search bar.

Pipe Down

Finally, it's worth mentioning one further setting, towards the bottom of the menu. Called Taskbar Tidbits, having this enables Cortana to greet you with a phrase in the search box – mainly to encourage you to use Cortana. It's not a big thing, but it could be irritating to some, but you can turn it off should you wish!

Exploring the Windows 10 Mail App

Long gone are the days of Microsoft Outlook Express being included with new releases of the OS, replaced instead by the Microsoft Mail app. This app first appeared in Windows 8, was vastly improved in 8.1 and has now been improved yet again for Windows 10.

New Mail Button

If you are not replying to an email, but rather starting a new email, you can do so in a couple of different ways. You can either click the New Mail button at the top of the Mail Menu or you can use the Ctrl-N. Both methods open a new email in the main window, with a blank recipient field.

Mail Menu

The left-hand menu, which can be minimised and expanded using the button at the top of the panel, contains all of your email accounts (those you have added to Windows Mail). Click on any of your email account headers and the individual folders, such as Inbox and Sent Items, are displayed here also.

Calendar View

You can open the Windows Calendar app directly from within the Mail app. Click the Mail app icon at the bottom of the Mail Menu panel and the calendar screen will open in a second window. If you have never used the Calendar app before, you will need to link it to an account.

Mail Settings

The settings for the Mail app allow you to easily add accounts, change how emails are displayed when they arrive, whether outgoing emails have a signature (which can be customised) added to them, as well as how you are notified of new emails in Windows 10.

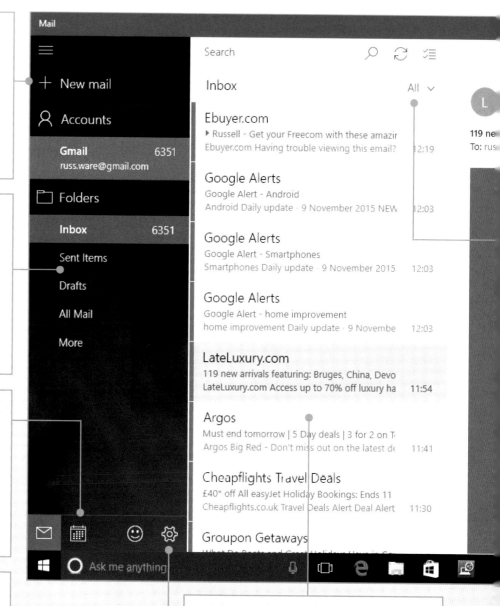

Mail Folder

The messages in whichever email folder you have selected are shown in this panel. By default, the most recent emails are at the top of the list. You can change how the emails are viewed, so that only unread or flagged emails are displayed, using the dropdown menu at the top of the inbox.

CUSTOMISE MAIL

You can customise how the Email app looks in a number of ways, from simple changes like choosing between a light and dark theme, to setting the overall colour and changing the background image for the app. To personalise the Mail app, click the Settings button and select "Personalisation".

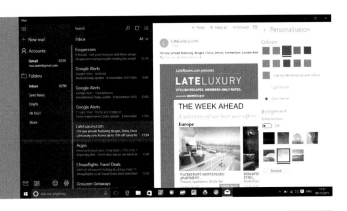

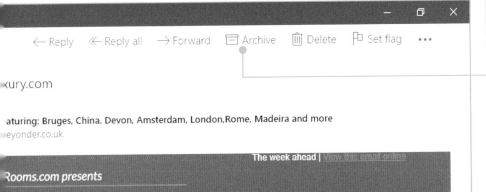

← Reply   ← Reply all   → Forward   ⊟ Archive   🗑 Delete   ⊞ Set flag   •••

...ury.com

...aturing: Bruges, China, Devon, Amsterdam, London, Rome, Madeira and more

...eyonder.co.uk

The week ahead | View this email online

Rooms.com presents

ATELUXURY

...ISH ESCAPES. MEMBERS-ONLY RATES.

by secret escapes

HE WEEK AHEAD

selection of our best new offers this week

...rope

...ATERFRONT MONTENEGRO
...ARTMENT...
...maris Apartments, Krtole Bay
...to 33% off   VIEW SALE

ROMANTIC BRUGES BREAK WITH EURO...
Hotel Prinsenhof, Belgium
Up to 39% off   VIEW SALE

∧ ▭ 📶 ◁ �)) 🗐 ENG   12:56
09/11/2015

Message Options

In a row along the top of the main message window are the message options. These include Reply, Reply All, Forward, Archive and Delete emails; more options can be seen by clicking the menu button to the right. The message options only appear when viewing a received message.

Message Tools

Roll over or click on any of the messages in your inbox, sent items or drafts folders and three icons will appear. These let you quickly Archive, Delete or Flag any message directly in the folder panel. Archived messages can be recovered at any time and returned to the inbox if required.

Main Message Window

When you start a new email or select an email in one of the mail folders, it will appear in the main message window. As you would normally, you can scroll down to view all of the messages shown. You can roll over the address in the To: field, to see more contact details.

Taskbar Icon

Whenever you open an app in Windows 10, a highlighted taskbar icon will appear at the bottom of the screen. This makes it easy to switch between multiple open apps, or to quickly see which apps are currently running. You can pin your most used apps to the taskbar by right-clicking and selecting Pin to Taskbar.

Set Up and Use Email and Accounts

Windows 10's new email client is a lot different from previous versions' apps such as Outlook Express in the late 1990s. But it's a relatively recent idea for us to have all our email in one place, whether it's our work account, a Hotmail or Outlook address or email from Gmail.

Meet Your New Email Client

Mail has been completely redesigned for Windows 10 and is wholly unrecognisable from the Windows 8 equivalent (that's a good thing). But even with these improvements, it still needs a bit of tweaking before it comes into its own.

Welcome As it says here, the idea behind the Mail app in Windows 10 is to gather all your emails together in one place to "simplify life a bit". The app is quite clever in how it handles email and it certainly differs to older apps such as Windows Live Mail and Outlook Express.

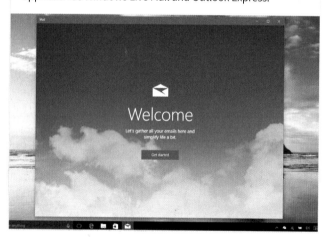

Account Type If you click Add Account, you can add accounts from many popular providers including Google, Yahoo and Apple's iCloud. You can also set up other more specialist accounts if you have the details. Finally, there's also an option to add a Microsoft Exchange account if your workplace uses that (including Office 365).

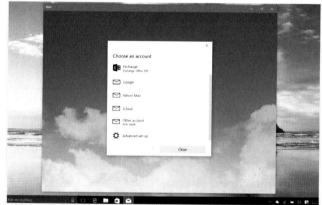

Default Account If you signed into Windows 10 with a Microsoft account, the Mail app will automatically pull this in if it's enabled for email. As you can see, you can also click Add Account if you have other email accounts you want to add (this can be from basically anywhere as long as it's your account).

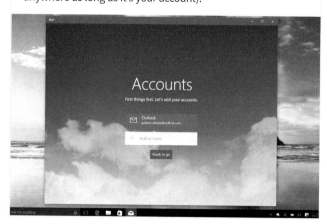

Advanced Setup If you need to select the Advanced Setup option, you can choose between the type of account you're setting up. Usually you'll select the Internet Email option – this includes accounts that use the POP3 or IMAP protocols to retrieve email (if your provider gives you the choice of which of those to use, select IMAP).

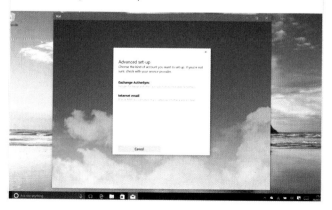

Google Accounts

If you're adding a Google account, you'll get this somewhat familiar pop-up appearing inviting you to enter your username and password. If you have Google's two-step authentication enabled, you'll get a text message to confirm your identity and you'll be asked to enter it.

Microsoft Accounts

As we said before, your Microsoft account will hopefully have already pulled in automatically. If not, you can add it manually. Just enter your email address and password. We looked at Microsoft accounts in more detail on page 8, but if you want to sign up afresh you can do that here too.

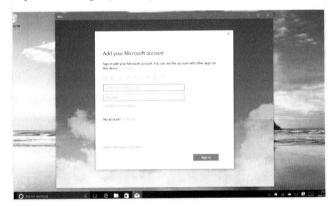

Your Inbox

Here's your inbox! Your email list is shown on the left, with the contents of each email appearing on the right. We have three new emails here, designated by the blue colour. You can also search for any emails using the search box at the top – this works much more quickly than in older apps.

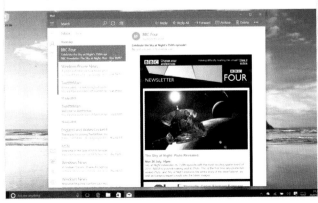

Writing a Mail

There's also a Refresh button as well as a Select mode, so you can select various emails (with a view to moving or deleting them). Now we've clicked the Forward button along the top to forward this email. As you can see, this has created a draft under the original email on the left.

Insert Attachment

Emails are 'grouped' like this in Mail, meaning that if you and a friend have a conversation, all the emails will be grouped together so that they're easy to retrieve. You'll notice we're still composing our email here, and we've clicked the Attach button to select an attachment.

Sent Mail

This is what a sent mail looks like. As you can see, it's now 'nested' under our original email and the sender is me (or you). You're able to look at just sent items in your folder still, and we'll show you how to do that in a few steps.

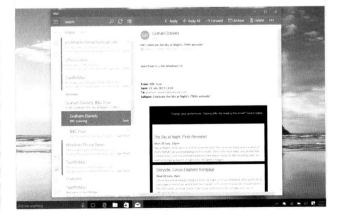

Email

Edit Text

As well as just writing simple plain text emails, there are plenty more editing functions in Mail, which we'll check out in the next few steps. Using the Format tab at the top of the editing window, you can change selected text – here we've used bold to highlight a particular phrase.

Apply Styles

There are also various pre-defined styles you can apply to text – useful if you're writing a long email and you need to have sub-headings or headlines in the text. These work very similarly to styles in Microsoft Office; styles that you might use for a report or essay.

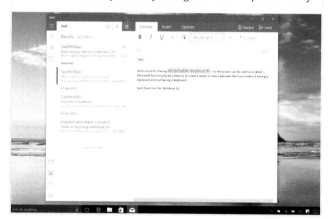

Define Styles

You can browse through these styles using the drop-down arrow next to the style selection box. As well as fairly standard styles, there are some other ways you can get text to stand out including quotes and what are called 'Intense' styles, which place quotes in between parallel lines to encourage reading.

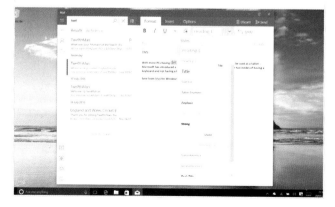

More Text Options

As well as styles, Bold, Italic and Underline, there are other ways you can make text stand out or add emphasis. As in Word, you can have subscript or superscript text or add highlighting (quite useful for quick editing of paragraphs in emails). Finally, you can clear the formatting of any selected text.

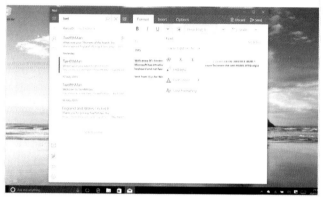

Change Colour

You're able to easily change the colour of the text in your email and, while you still have a limited range to choose from, you've still got a lot of choice (far more than in many other apps, anyway). Strangely Windows chooses to take most of these colours from your current Windows theme. No, we're not sure why, either.

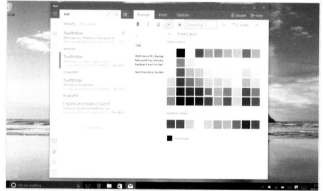

Inserting Images

As well as the button to include attachments, the Insert tab features a Picture button so you can insert an image into your email, as opposed to just sending it as an attached file. Once inserted, you can select it with your mouse and adjust its size (drag the corners as you can see here).

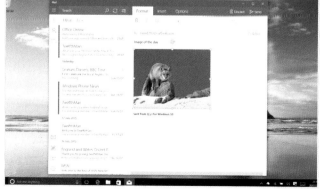

Spelling Options   Before you send an email, you can always spell check it – this is integrated into Mail under the Options tab. You can select the language you need (you might be emailing a hotel in France so using French, for example) and correct any spelling errors as you go.

Change Zoom   If the text in emails is too small for you, you can zoom in to your messages – again, this is also accessed through the … menu. A handy keyboard shortcut for zooming in is Ctrl-+ to zoom in or use Ctrl and – to zoom out. This actually works in most apps, including many web browsers, too!

Email Menu   As well as the basic reply, reply all, forward, archive and delete commands at the top of each email, there's also this extra menu – just click the … button. You can move to the next email or previous message if you want to do that, but crucially you can also move your email into a folder.

Right-Click   Even if you're not actually looking at a particular email, you can still perform numerous actions on it. You can right-click on emails to move, archive or delete them or mark them as read/unread. If you're deleting emails, you can also just select them and use the delete key (we find this is actually the easiest way).

Move Folder   If you chose to move your email in the previous step, you'll see this browser view which enables you to add your email to an existing folder. You can always create a new folder for storing emails in particular categories. If you just want to remove your email from the inbox but still keep it, use Archive.

Print It Off   From this menu you can also print off emails – this will open the now-standard Windows print dialog box which is now black (presumably to make the predominantly white print preview stand out). You can select to print off the whole email or just the first page, as well as browse through the pages using the controls at the top.

86	**Internet Safety and Security Tips**

Learn some simple and effective ways to make going online safer.

94	**Using the Windows Defender Tools**

Discover the built-in tools for making Windows 10 safer and more secure.

102	**Antivirus and Security Software**

Discover some of the completely free security software available for PC.

Windows 10 Security and Privacy

There seems to be hardly a day that goes by without some news of data being hacked. Some of the most important elements of Windows 10, and something everyone who uses a computer online should know more about, are the security and privacy features. From Windows sign-in and Family options to Windows Defender, this stuff is important!

86 Internet Safety and Security Tips

90 Security Risks for Windows 10 Users

92 Manage Your Privacy Settings

94 Using the Windows Defender Tools

96 Creating Backups of Your Files

98 Back Up with a Recovery Drive

100 How to Use the Dynamic Lock

101 How to Use Night Light Mode

102 Top Ten Antivirus and Security Packages

Internet Safety and Security Tips

Keeping your computer, and the personal data which may be stored on it, safe and private is not as big a challenge as it might seem. The News is full of stories about "Hackers" but the chances of your personal computer being directly targeted are very small. What is more important is to understand how you should interact with websites and the simple ways to ensure your data is as secure as possible.

Online Safety Basics

The best and most effective way to protect your privacy, security and the continued smooth operation of your Windows device is to install a good security and antivirus app. There are some good free apps available, such as Avast Antivirus or AVG, as well as more comprehensive security software suites that you'll have to pay to use, such as Kaspersky Internet Security.

Do Your Homework Before Buying Online

While the majority of online retailers are perfectly reputable, there are a few that are less than honest. If you're not sure you can check out the company's reputation on shopper comparison sites such as Pricerunner or Kelkoo or simply type the name into Google along with terms such as "fraud", "rip off" or "complaint". See what others have been saying about them and if they have a lot of negative feedback then take your money elsewhere.

Read Your Bank Statements

Whether you have printed statements or you do all of your banking online, it's a good idea to check your bank and credit card account regularly. If you see any suspicious payments that you don't recognise, contact your bank and get them to look into it. Most credit cards offer protection against online fraud but they can only act on it if you report it.

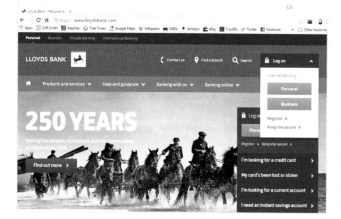

If it Sounds too Good to be True...

If you receive an email, text or chat message telling you that you've won millions on a lottery you've never entered, that a deceased relative you've never heard of has left you a fortune or that some foreign businessman wants to move a huge sum of money and needs your help to do so, don't bother replying; simply delete the message at once. This type of scam is known as an "advance fee fraud" or 419 scam, after the Nigerian penal code law that it contravenes.

ONLINE PASSWORD TIPS

It can be tempting to use the same or similar passwords for several different websites or apps. This can be a bad idea, particularly if your chosen password is something easy to guess such as your name or date of birth. Here are a few tips to consider when creating passwords.

1. Keep them Unique
Having a unique password for each website or app you are required to log in to is a very good idea, particularly for things like email and online banking. Although security on a banking website is likely to be very good, if you use the same password on a website with less stringent security, you risk it being compromised on one and used to gain access to the other.

2. Keep them Random
Try to avoid using anything that is easy to guess, including personal information like your name, date of birth or address. These things are all very easy to discover and often the first things someone will try to get into your accounts. Also avoid, if possible, using real words or sequential strings of numbers (e.g. 123456789).

3. The Longer, the Better
Short passwords are much easier to crack than long ones, so be sure to avoid anything less than eight characters and, if possible, go for something at least ten characters long. There are 4000 times more possible combinations of ten letters and numbers than there are for eight letters and numbers.

4. Use a Mixture
Once you start adding in symbols and mixed case letters, along with numbers, into your passwords, the possible variations rise to over 6 quadrillion (for an eight character password). The password A1z7yDbP is many thousands of times more secure than a1z7ydbp.

PASSWORD MANAGERS

For most people, keeping a written list of their passwords is perfectly okay as long as you make sure that it is not left in plain sight on your desk, etc. Even keeping a text document on your computer with you passwords listed is not usually a risk; just don't call the file 'Passwords' and leave in on the desktop. A much safer way is to use a good Password Manager. These simple bits of software let you store your passwords in a locked file on your computer. As long as you have a very good password to get into the manager, your other passwords will be safe. You then only need to remember one password, instead of 10 or 20. Lastpass is a very good and free example of a password manager.

WHAT ARE COOKIES?

Cookies (or HTML Cookies) are small files used by websites to recognise individual users; or rather, recognise their computer. When you visit a website, a cookie is stored in a temporary folder on your computer. When you next visit that site, the cookie will be checked for. Different sites use cookies to store different information but a good example is information in a form being automatically filled when visiting a site you have used recently to order something.

Almost all modern browsers, including Internet Explorer and Chrome, allow you to block cookies from being downloaded. However it is worth remembering that many websites now need cookies to work properly and so blocking them could mean your browsing experience is a frustrating one. Cookies are nothing to be afraid of; they are simply used to make the Internet work better.

Enable/Disable Cookies in Chrome

As mentioned you can disable cookies in most modern browsers. Here's how to disable cookies in the current version of Google Chrome.

Step 1 To enable cookies in Chrome, click the wrench icon or menu button in the top right corner of the browser window. Select Settings, scroll to the bottom and click Show advanced settings. Now click Content settings in the "Privacy" section.

Step 2 Select Allow local data to be set to allow both first-party and third-party cookies. If you only want to accept first-party cookies, check the box next to "Block all third-party cookies without exception."

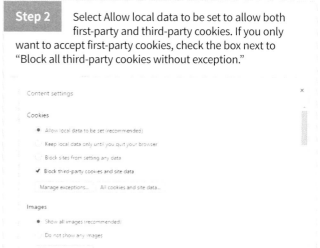

AVOID PHISHING ATTEMPTS

Phishing is the process of trying to find private information such as PIN numbers, passwords and user names by trickery. Sometimes spammers create fake websites that look like the login pages of well-known websites. When you enter your email and password on one of these pages, the spammer records your information and keeps it.

An increasingly common form of phishing is to randomly send out emails pertaining to be from banks; they ask the recipient to follow a link and confirm their online banking username and password. This is usually as a "security precaution" or because there is some supposed problem with your account.

When someone has been phished, their email account will often start automatically sending messages or links to a large number of their friends. These messages or links are often advertisements telling friends to check out videos or products. If you think your friend's account was phished, tell them to change their password and run antivirus software on their computer.

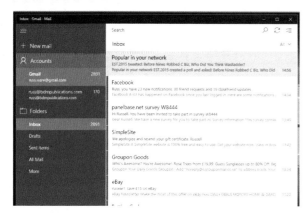

CYBER BULLYING

Sadly bullying isn't only confined to the playground or classroom any more. Cyber Bullying is when a child (or even an adult) is bullied via text message, email, social networks or other online means.

The best way to deal with a cyber bully on a social network is to simply block that person, or not accept the friend request of someone who bullies you in real life. Although it may be tempting to reply to rude or abusive comments etc. it is usually better to just ignore the person. In some cases, bullies have created fake accounts on social networks pretending to be their victim. If you discover someone has created an account pretending to be you, report it immediately to the network's administrators. There is usually a button to "Report..." on the user profile page.

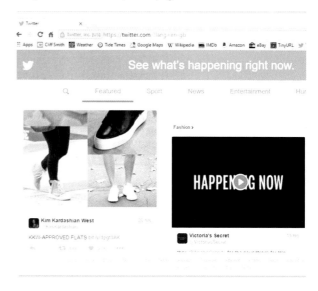

SOCIAL NETWORKS – ADVICE FOR PARENTS

As parents ourselves, we understand the pressure that many people feel to let their children use the Internet and social networks in particular. Many social networking sites including Facebook, don't allow children under 13 years of age to have accounts.

Unfortunately there is little they can do to stop a child below that age entering false details. Rather than a blanket ban on using the Internet and social networks and potentially have your child visit them behind your back, perhaps a better way to keep your child safe is to understand the dangers yourself and make sure your children understand them as well.

Get Involved
Take the next step and create an account for yourself on the social networks your child uses. This not only helps you to understand how things work and what features could be a potential problem but it also allows you to more easily see what your child is doing on there. You will be far better informed when asking questions about the site, than if you simply read about it.

Privacy Settings
Almost all of the well-known social networking sites offer several levels of privacy settings. Ensure your child selects the strongest privacy setting available when they create their account. This will help to make sure that their personal information is only seen by people they want to share it with. Be aware however, that some sites are totally open to the public.

Internet Safety Tips

• Make sure that you don't publish personal information such as your location, email address, phone number or date of birth on social networks.

• Be careful about what images and messages you post, even among trusted friends – once they are online they can be shared widely and are extremely difficult to get removed.

• Encourage your family to talk to you if they come across anything they find offensive or upsetting. Keep a record of anything abusive or offensive received and report any trouble to the site administrators.

• Try to be aware of online scams. Offers that seem too good to be true usually are and be aware that clicking links you are unsure about can be unwise.

Blocking People on Facebook

There may be a time when you want to block another Facebook user. There are several reasons why you might want to do this, from unwanted messages and rude status updates, to phishing attempts or spam.

Step 1 Click on the account menu at the top of your profile and select Privacy Settings. Scroll down to Blocked People and Apps and click Manage Blocking.

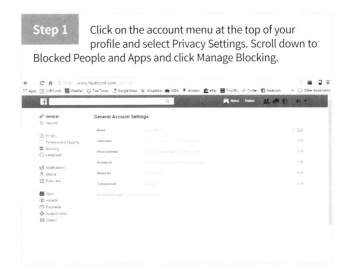

Step 2 Enter the name or email address of the person you want to block and click Block. People will not be notified when you block them.

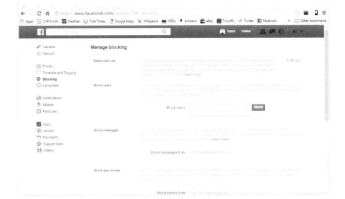

Step 3 If you can't find someone using this method, try going to the person's profile (timeline) and selecting Report/Block This Person from the drop-down menu at the top of the page.

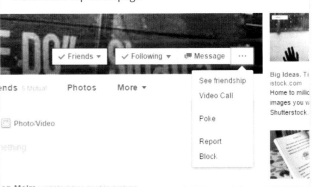

Security Risks for Windows 10 Users

There are more security risks for your computer than just the common, run-of-the-mill virus. The amount of digital activity the average person gets through over the course of a week has increased significantly in just a few years and with it comes a legion of security related issues.

Understanding the Risks

This is not a definitive list of the possible threats available for the Windows user but here are ten modern risks that you face every time you power up your PC.

Risk 1 – Viruses
Viruses have been around for as long as computers. They've moved on from simply displaying the name of the coder on the monitor, a kind of virtual vandalism, and now can disable and wipe the data off a hard drive in mere seconds.

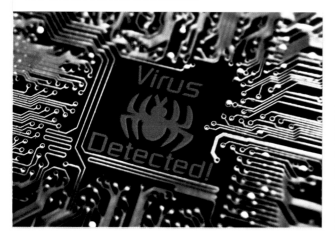

Risk 3 – Worms
A worm is a type of virus but it behaves differently, in that it's goal isn't to alter or destroy system files. Rather, it's designed to replicate itself continuously until all the resources and space on the system are consumed. A bit of a nightmare for the system administrator.

Risk 2 – Ransomware
Earlier in the year the UK was gripped in the clutches of the WannaCry ransomware infection. This particular infection exploited a vulnerability in Windows and quickly spread throughout the NHS and other organisations, locking and encrypting the data on a computer until money was sent to those who unleashed it to the world.

Risk 4 – Trojans
The Trojan horse is a program that masquerades as a legitimate application but in actual fact contains code that allows a hacker remote access to your computer. Like the legend of the wooden horse the Greeks used, once inside your computer it opens and create an opening for the hacker.

Risk 5 – Spyware

Spyware invades computers usually through freeware or shareware downloads, which is why you should always download a program from a reputable source. The intent of spyware is to collect information about the user and report it back to those who wrote it.

Risk 6 – Adware

Adware is very similar to spyware, in that one of its goals is to monitor the user. However, adware usually goes one step further and bombards the user with Internet pop-up advertising, usually when they open their browser or a new tab. The advertising can be tame, or it can be extremely offensive.

Risk 7 – Hacking

While Hollywood would have you visualise the lifestyle of a hacker as something that's quite alluring, in truth it's quite the opposite. The average user is generally under the radar where a hacker is concerned. They're mostly after the corporations or famous people, but you can have your computer hacked by a neighbour, for example.

Risk 8 – Social Engineering

A relatively modern term in the history of computer security, social engineering will have the user deceived into giving away personal information or allowing a scammer into their systems. The recent spate of calls from people claiming to be from the likes of Microsoft or a security firm, are a prime example.

Risk 9 – Phishing

Much in the same vein as social engineering, phishing is the act of obtaining sensitive information (bank details usually) about a user by being disguised as a trustworthy source. Phishing on social media sites such as Facebook, Twitter and so on are on the rise.

Risk 10 – Rootkits

Rootkits are virus-like programs that are activated before the computer's antivirus and security suites are started when booting Windows. They can change the way a security suite looks at files, allowing a virus to hide in plain sight and not be detected by the system's security measures.

Manage Your Privacy Settings

Being in control of security on your computer is important but almost as important is being able to control your privacy. Microsoft recently launched a web-based privacy dashboard and this has now become available to everyone in the Creators update. Manage privacy settings across multiple devices using a single account.

The Privacy Dashboard

The privacy dashboard is web-based rather than in the settings and it allows you to manage multiple devices from a single interface, as long as you are logged in to a single account.

Step 1 Open your browser and navigate to www. account.microsoft.com/privacy. If prompted, use your Microsoft account details to log in. You will be logged in to the privacy overview page that lets you quickly see what privacy settings the dashboard contains and controls.

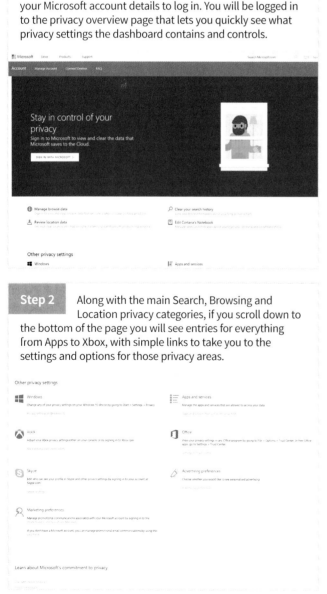

Step 2 Along with the main Search, Browsing and Location privacy categories, if you scroll down to the bottom of the page you will see entries for everything from Apps to Xbox, with simple links to take you to the settings and options for those privacy areas.

Step 3 Click on one of the main categories, Search, Browsing, Location or Cortana, and you will see more information. This could include a list of searches you have made or websites visited (in Edge only, not other browsers), interests Cortana has saved for you or locations you have been.

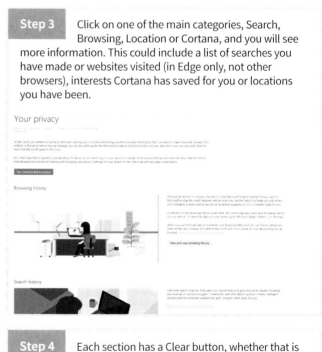

Step 4 Each section has a Clear button, whether that is clearing browsing history, search history and so on. It is next to a warning that states clearing data will stop Windows being able to provide you with accurate and relevant information. You need to decide what is more important, privacy or recommendations.

Step 5 Another useful privacy section in the dashboard is the Advertising Preferences. This lets you control whether personalised adverts are shown to you in the Edge browser. Some of the ads you may receive on Microsoft websites and apps are tailored to your previous activities and searches.

Step 6 There is also a browser tool that lets you choose if the adverts you see come from companies other than Microsoft. Click the option under More Choices and wait for the Digital Advertising Alliance scan to finish. You can then choose from the list to see adverts from different advert providers.

Where Can I Learn More about Advertising on Microsoft Websites and Apps?

Microsoft partners with AOL, AppNexus and other third party service providers to help present customised content and display advertisements on MSN, Outlook.com and other websites and apps. Microsoft also delivers search ads to Bing and our search syndication partners. Learn more about Microsoft's privacy practices here. You can learn more about interest-based ads from AOL and AppNexus in their privacy statements: AOL and AppNexus.

What Choices Do I Have About Interest-Based Advertising?

On this page, you can opt out of receiving interest-based advertising from Microsoft.

You can also opt out of receiving interest-based advertising from all self-regulatory members, including Microsoft, AOL, AppNexus and other third party ad networks, at the following sites:

- In the US: Digital Advertising Alliance (DAA).
- In Europe: European Interactive Digital Advertising Alliance (EDAA).
- In Canada: Ad Choices Digital Advertising Alliance of Canada (DAAC).

You can control interest-based advertising in Windows apps by turning off the advertising ID in Windows Settings.

More choices

Questions?

Personalised ads in this browser

ON

Control the "personalised ads" setting for this web browser.

Learn more

Personalised ads wherever I use my Microsoft account

OFF

Control the "personalised ads" setting that applies when you are signed in on any computer or device with your Microsoft account, including Windows, Windows phone, Xbox and other devices.

Learn more

Personalised ads in Windows

Privacy Settings

There are, of course, still privacy options in the main settings app in Windows 10. This is generally added to and improved with each OS update.

General Privacy Privacy has its own section within the settings; here there are many different categories covering everything from Location to Background Apps. Click on each of the privacy categories to see the options within that category. Use the slider switches to allow or block privacy actions.

Account Info Apps are able to access very basic personal settings such as your name and account information. This is so they can sign you in automatically to your Windows account for things like Xbox Live or the Windows Store. You can turn this off wholesale or on an app by app basis.

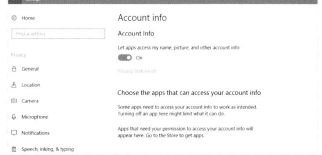

Messaging Apps We're using Windows 10 on a laptop here but if we had a tablet with a SIM card we would be able to get control over which apps were able to send messages over SMS and MMS. You probably want this to be restricted to just your Messaging app; most apps really shouldn't have access to your texts.

Background Apps You can control which apps you allow to run in the background. If you're on a laptop or desktop this probably won't be that big an issue, but you may want to turn these off on tablet devices to conserve power. Some apps you may not use, like Get Office, really don't need to run in the background.

Using the Windows Defender Tools

Thanks to a fairly recent update, Windows Defender, the preinstalled security tool for Windows 10, is better than ever. Defender now includes cloud-based protection and automatic analysis of suspicious software or files. You can even run a powerful offline scan that can pick up nasties that a normal scan may not.

Set Up Defender

By default, Windows Defender should already by running but if you are using a PC that has had antivirus software on in the past, parts of it may have been disabled.

Step 1 The first thing to do is check that Defender is already running. You can quickly check this by clicking on 'Show hidden icons' (the small arrow button) at the right-hand end of the taskbar. If you see the Defender shield logo, you are protected. At least, you are protected partially.

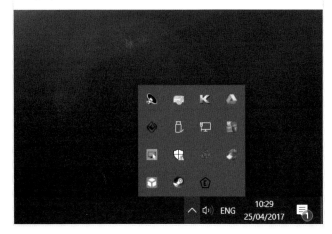

Step 2 Now it's time to check out the Defender settings and features. You can right-click on the icon in the hidden icons pop-up, and then click Open. You can also, in the search box on the taskbar, type Defender and then select Windows Defender from the list of results.

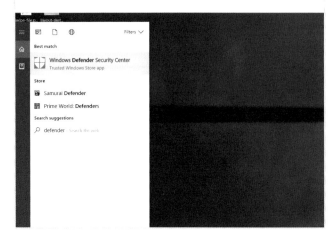

Step 3 Since the Creators update of April '17, Defender is much more in keeping, design-wise, with the rest of the Windows 10 interface, although it still opens in a separate window. The Defender Security Centre is split into several sections, including antivirus, firewall and device performance.

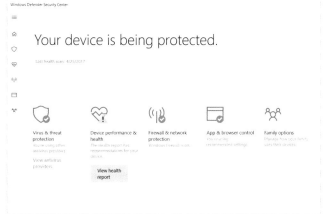

Step 4 Below each of the section icons, you can see basic info about that section, including whether it is currently enabled or not. Click on any of the section titles and you are able to see more information, along with any options available for that particular part of Defender.

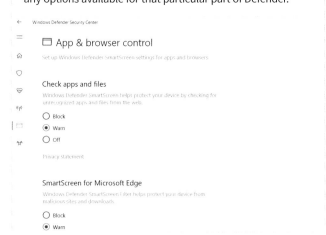

Running a Virus Scan

You can scan your PC for viruses in a couple of different ways with Windows Defender. Click the Virus & Threat Protection icon to get started.

Step 1 If you are using a third-party antivirus program, such as Kaspersky or AVG, it will say so at the top of the window. If you want to check exactly which, click the link 'View antivirus providers'. This opens the Windows Control Panel. Click Security to open the panel and look for Virus Protection.

Step 2 You can still use Defender to scan for viruses, with or without other antivirus software present. Back in the Virus & Threat Protection window, click the Quick scan button to get started. A progress bar appears, along with some details of files scanned and time elapsed.

Step 3 You can, if you are not sure the Quick scan is enough, perform an offline scan. This is a much deeper scan and certainly takes longer to perform. It is, however, much more likely to find some of the more devious viruses and other threats. Click Advanced scan and select offline scan > Scan now.

Step 4 The other options here let you check for protection updates, as well as change the Virus & Threat protection settings; for example whether real-time protection is on. You can also choose files or software to exclude from scans and change the notification settings for Windows Defender.

Windows Firewall

A firewall is often the first defence against viruses and other Internet nasties, so make sure you at least use the one provided by Windows 10.

Step 1 You should always run Windows Firewall even if you have another firewall turned on. Turning off Windows Firewall might make your device, and your network if you have one, more vulnerable to unauthorised access.

Step 2 To turn Windows Firewall on or off, select the Start button, open Windows Defender Security Centre > Firewall & network protection, choose a network profile and then under Windows Firewall, turn it on or off.

Creating Backups of Your Files

Windows 10 is a very stable and reliable operating system but disaster can still strike on occasion, either via an internal problem or an external one. Being able to, and remembering to, create backups of your system and important files is an important skill, one that can save you hours or possibly days of frustration and worry.

Using File History

To back up using File History, you will need a secondary storage drive. This can be an internal or network-connected hard drive or a removable flash drive. We are using a flash drive.

Step 1 The first thing to do is to make sure that your storage drive has enough free space on it. If it is brand new, you don't need to worry about this step but if the drive has been used previously, you should check. Insert the drive into a USB port and open File Explorer.

Step 2 You should see the drive listed with a drive letter, for example: USB Drive (F:). Right-click on the drive name and select Properties from the menu that appears. You can now see how much space is remaining on your flash drive and how much is available in total.

Step 3 Assuming you have a good amount of storage space on the drive, you can begin the process of backing up files. File History backs up copies of files that are in the Documents, Music, Pictures, Videos and Desktop folders and the OneDrive files available offline on your PC.

Step 4 If you have files elsewhere that you want to back up using File History, you'll need to move them to one of these folders before you start to back up. In most cases this can be done using cut and paste (Ctrl + C and Ctrl + V) or by right-clicking the icon of the file and selecting Copy and the same on the folder using Paste.

Step 5 Now open the main settings app in Windows 10 and click on Update & Security > Backup. Click the 'Add a drive' button and you will hopefully see your USB drive detected. Click on the drive in the list to select it. This is now designated as your backup drive and can be left in the USB port.

Step 7 Back in the Backup screen of the settings, click on More options. This shows you exactly which folders are backed up and how large the backup is. Your files will not be backed up straight away with File History but you can click the 'Back up now' button to initiate it.

Step 6 File History regularly backs up versions of your files in the Documents, Music, Pictures, Videos and Desktop folders and the OneDrive files available offline on your PC. Over time, you will have a complete history of your files. If the originals are lost, damaged or deleted, you can restore them.

Step 8 You can change how often your computer backs up, from every 10 minutes to once a day. You can also choose how long backups are kept before they are overwritten by new ones. This ranges from one month to forever, although you can also set it so that they are kept until space is needed.

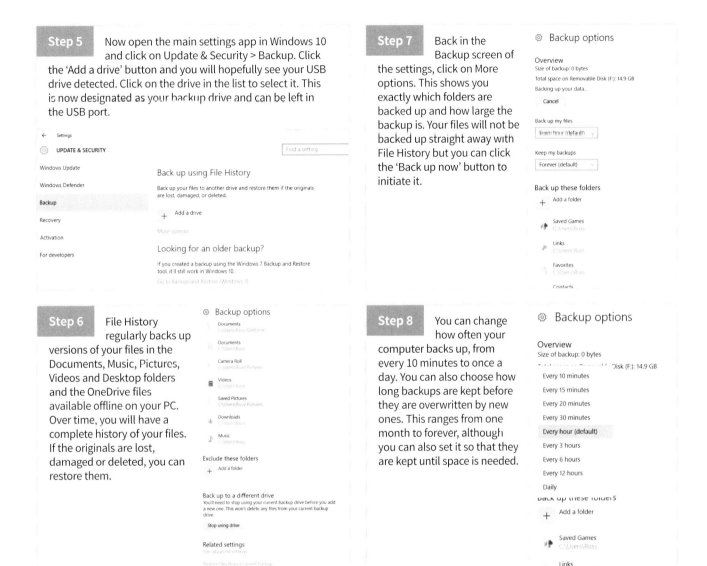

Restoring Backups

It is no good having your files backed up if you don't know how to restore them after a system failure. You will need your storage drive plugged in to your PC to restore files.

Step 1 In the search field of the taskbar, type "restore your files with file history" and click on the result shown. Enter the name of the file you're looking for in the search box or use the left and right arrows to browse through different versions of your folders and files.

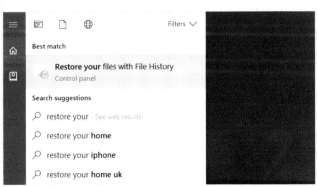

Step 2 Select what you want to restore to its original location and then select the Restore button. If you want to restore your files to a different location than the original, press and hold or right-click the Restore button; select Restore To and then choose a new location.

Back Up with a Recovery Drive

A recovery drive is one of the best ways to ensure that you don't lose everything on your computer in the event of a critical malfunction. It can help you both troubleshoot and fix problems, even if the PC won't start as it normally would. All you need is a blank, formatted USB flash drive (sometimes called a thumb drive) and this step-by-step guide.

Creating the Recovery Drive

Creating a recovery drive is a relatively simple process, although it takes a bit of time, but one which could save a lot of frustration in the future.

Step 1 The first thing you need to do is find a USB drive that is large enough and then make sure it is ready to be used. The USB drive you decide to use won't be able to be used for anything else like storing other files, etc. so make sure it is a spare, or bought specifically for the task.

Step 2 A basic Windows 10 recovery file will be less than 500MB but if you choose to include system files in the backup (recommended), so you can use it to reinstall Windows, you will need much more space. A basic recovery drive can be as small as 1GB but a full recovery drive needs to be at least 8GB.

Step 3 Your USB drive needs to be wiped of everything currently on it before the recovery drive is created. You can do this during the set up process later or you can format it yourself right now: a useful thing to know how to do. Insert your USB drive into a free USB slot on in your computer.

Step 4 Open the File Explorer on your computer and you should see the USB flash drive listed in the sidebar. It will probably be labelled as the (E:) or (F:) drive. Right-click on the drive label and select Format from the action menu. Leave the settings as default (should be FAT32) and then click Start.

Step 5 You should now be ready to create your recovery drive. In the search field, type "Recovery Drive" and select the Create a Recovery Drive result. In newer versions of Windows 10, you might also be able to find the Recovery Drive in the main apps list, opened by clicking the Start menu button.

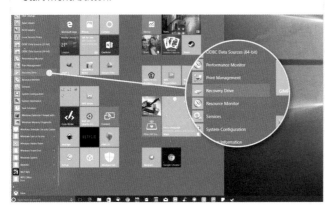

Step 6 Allow the software to "make changes to this PC" and the setup wizard will open. This first screen is where you choose whether you want to back up system files with the recovery drive, so you can use it to reinstall Windows 10. If you do, tick the checkbox and then click Next.

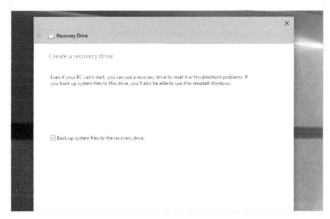

Step 7 After a few moments, you will be asked to select the USB flash drive you wish to use. If you only have one USB drive inserted, it will be the only one shown and will be automatically selected. You are reminded again how much storage space the drive needs, and that all existing data will be wiped.

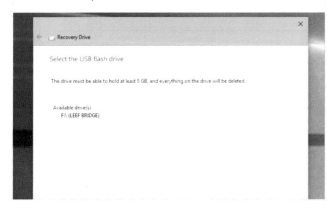

Step 8 Click Create on the next screen and the process will begin. This may take a while to complete, so go make a coffee and leave it to run. A progress bar shows how far along it is, should you need to check. Do not remove the USB drive, or turn off your computer, before the process finishes.

Step 9 When the process is complete, you should be prompted to delete the recovery partition on your PC, to save some space; as long as you plan to keep your recovery drive, this is safe to do. If you are not sure, you can leave the recovery partition in place; it can be deleted at a later date if you wish.

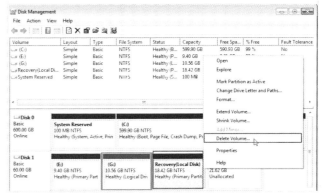

Step 10 If you did not already have a recovery partition on your computer, you won't see this step. You will simply be informed that the recovery drive is ready, and to click Finish. Remove the USB drive from your computer and put it somewhere safe. It is a good idea to label the drive so it is not reused.

How to Use the Dynamic Lock

The Creators update for Windows 10 introduces several new tools and features, including Dynamic Lock. This allows you to have more control over the security of your Windows device, with even less effort. It is designed to detect a trusted device nearby and lock and unlock the computer as it moves away or comes close.

Setting Up Dynamic Lock

Dynamic Lock works by sensing the proximity of a paired device, such as your smartphone. In this example, the first thing we need to do is pair with our phone. Pairing with other Bluetooth devices will be almost exactly the same as shown here.

Step 1 Dynamic Lock will only work if your PC has Bluetooth connectivity. This usually means a laptop, which makes sense as these more portable devices are more in need of security measures. Open Settings > Devices > Bluetooth & Other devices. Turn Bluetooth on using the slider switch and do this on your phone as well.

Step 2 Once you see the phone listed under available devices, select it and pair to it. If you can't see your device listed, you may need to update your USB drivers for your PC: look for Bluetooth USB Module in Device Manager. Once paired successfully, you are ready to begin setting up and using Dynamic lock.

Step 3 Go to Settings > Accounts > Sign-in Options and scroll down to see the Dynamic Lock section. Check the box that says 'Allow Windows to detect when you are away and automatically lock the device'. Hopefully, assuming Bluetooth is working, that is all you need to do to start using the feature.

Step 4 Dynamic Lock does have some limitations at the moment, although these might be ironed out. The lock will not kick in until 30 seconds after it detects the Bluetooth signal has moved away, and if someone jumps on your computer within that time and starts to use it, it doesn't activate at all.

How to Use Night Light Mode

Most screens give off blue light, which is known to activate our brains and keep us awake. It can also cause tired or sore eyes. The latest version of Windows 10 (the recent Creators Update) has added a Night Light mode to the settings. This setting, when enabled, will take much of the blue light out of the monitor.

Set Up and Use Night Light

There are a couple of different ways you can use Night Light mode and a few settings that can be used to make it perfect for your display and personal preference.

Step 1 To turn Night Light on, head in to Settings > System > Display. At the top of the display settings you will see the Night Light slider switch and you can simply click the slider to turn Night Light on as you need it. If you don't see it, you will need to check that you have updated Windows 10 with the Creators update.

Step 2 As soon as you click the slider you see the screen change. Some of the blue light is stripped out and the colour shifts towards the red spectrum. If you don't see a change, it may be that the feature is configured to activate during certain set hours (between 19:00 and 7:00, for example).

Step 3 Click Night Light Settings and then Turn on now, if you just want the feature activated. Alternatively, you can set a schedule, so that your device switches to Night Light mode at the same time each evening. Click 'Schedule night light' and choose the on and off times using the clock interface.

Step 4 You can also alter the colour temperature of the display change when Night Light is activated. Some displays may respond better to the default change than others, so if you think you need more blue light blocked out (or less), use the colour slider to change the amount until it suits you.

⚙ Night light settings

Screens emit blue light, which can keep you up at night. Night light displays warmer colors to help you sleep.

On until 07:00

Turn off now

Color temperature at night

Schedule

Schedule night light

On

Turn on Location services to schedule night light at sunset.

Exploring the Windows Store

Windows 10 comes with great built-in apps including Skype and OneDrive but that's just the beginning. The Store has loads more to help you stay in touch and get things done, plus more games and entertainment than ever before – many of them free!

Category Tabs

Just as with other online app stores, the Windows Store features several different download categories. These include Apps, Games, Music and Films. Each category has its own home screen, which displays: Most Popular, Top Free and Trending sections.

Featured Apps

The Featured Apps slider will display those apps or games that are trending or have been particularly popular. This display is constantly updated and is a good way of finding out what other Windows 10 users are using and playing.

Software Charts

These links take you to lists of the most popular and most downloaded apps and games on the Windows Store. Once you click on one of the links, you can further refine the chart using the links on the left-hand sidebar. Filters include Top Free, Top Paid, Best Rated and New & Rising.

Apps and Games

As you scroll down the main page of the App, Game, Music or Film home screens, you will see additional sections showing Most Popular, Top Free, etc. If you want to see all of the apps in a particular section, click the "Show All" button on the right.

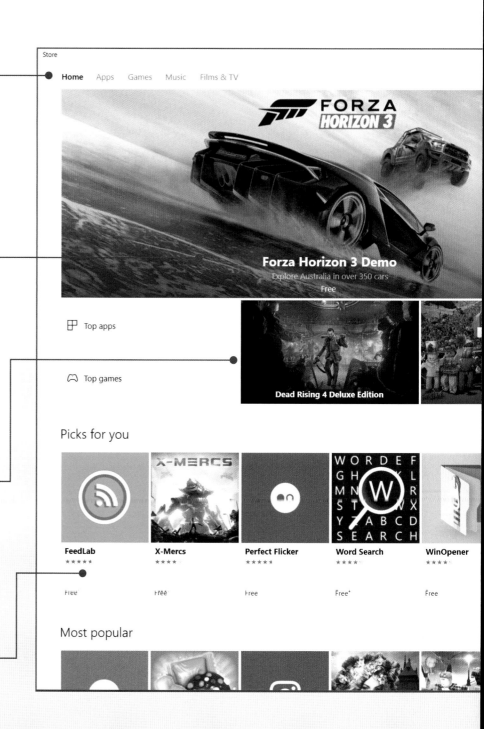

APP INFO SCREEN

Once you have found the app or game you want to install, click on the icon to open the app info screen. This screen displays the average app score, user reviews, similar app suggestions, as well as a list of features and updates. Click the Free, Buy or Try button to install the software.

Downloads/Updates

If there is an update or new download available for any app you currently have installed on your computer, a notification will appear here. The number shows how many updates/app downloads are waiting. Click the arrow and select the required action (update, retry etc.).

Store Settings

Click the small Account icon here to see the store settings option. Here you will find details of the Microsoft account currently being used, along with several sliders used to control things like automatic app updates. You can also control who can install new apps on your PC.

Search Bar

You can use the main search bar in the taskbar to search for apps, games, music and films in the Windows Store (store results will have the store icon next to them in the results list). Alternatively, you can search just inside the store by using this search bar.

Windows Store Offers

Periodically, the Windows Store will feature offers for its users. This could be a free Groove Music 30 day trial, or other download offers. Click on the link to read more about the offer and then follow the instructions to take advantage of it.

Using the Windows Store

There was a Windows Store inside Windows 8, but Microsoft has a new version inside Windows 10. That's because – like the new so-called 'Universal' apps - the Store will work across all Microsoft devices including Windows Phones and the Xbox One.

Take a Look Around

The great thing about the new Windows Store is that the quality of the apps has improved, so it's actually worth browsing. But aside from better apps, the whole experience of looking for new software has been improved in Windows 10.

Step 1 As well as being more responsive to use, the Windows Store has improved vastly in terms of content – as well as apps and games there are now movies to buy or rent and music to download. You can switch between the major sections using the buttons at the top of the window.

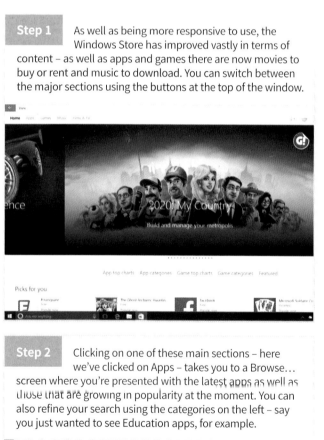

Step 2 Clicking on one of these main sections – here we've clicked on Apps – takes you to a Browse… screen where you're presented with the latest apps as well as those that are growing in popularity at the moment. You can also refine your search using the categories on the left – say you just wanted to see Education apps, for example.

Step 3 Each section also features charts of the most downloaded apps as well as curated app recommendations. Here the selection is reasonably uninspiring but presumably this would improve as you downloaded more apps. You can also easily flick through the top free and paid apps.

Step 4 As in many Windows 10 apps, there's a search box in the top right. The search will pick up results from across the Store, whatever you search for. Here we've found a film we'd like to see. This page is roughly the same whether you're looking at a game, movie or app.

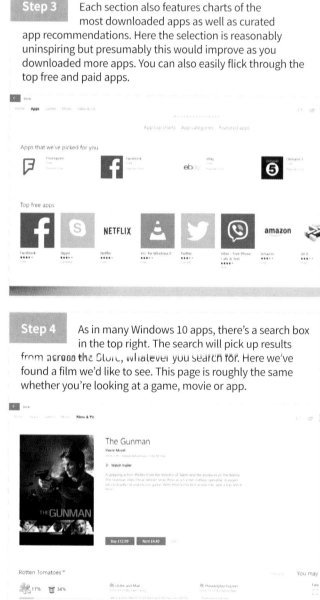

Step 5 Here's what it looks like if you go to an album page in the Music section. Like the movie page in the previous step, there's a Buy link but no button to rent as there is with movie downloads. With movies you can also choose to watch the trailer, while you can preview a snippet of music.

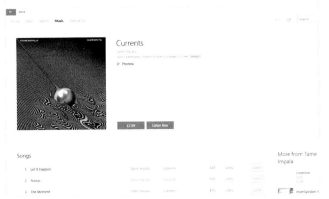

Step 6 You're also able to buy single tracks, too – here they're 99p. At every stage the Windows Store will select other appropriate content for you to look at (often from the back catalogue or related artists), while you can also click any artist or album name to go to the relevant page.

Step 7 Should you wish to, you're also able to join Microsoft's subscription music service Groove Music Pass. We've talked more about the service in our Groove Music app tutorial, but essentially it gives you unlimited access to the Windows Store music catalogue and you can listen on basically any device, including Android and iPhone. There's a 30-day trial but the service usually costs £9 per month.

Step 8 You don't to pay for most apps on the Windows Store. There are stacks of apps you can get hold of for free. Each app has a helpful star rating and user reviews, so you can always see which apps aren't ones that are recommended by others.

Step 9 When you download an app or other content, it will be added to your download queue. Apps will download and then install relatively quickly but other content – especially HD movies – could take longer. You can also click the blue Check for Updates button to check for app updates, though these will install automatically.

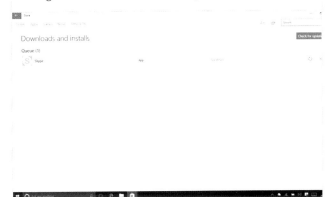

Step 10 Paid-for apps use your credit or debit card. This is all connected to your Microsoft account and you can view your current account and billing information at account.microsoft.com. You can have multiple payment options should you choose to. At the Microsoft account site you're also able to view what Microsoft services (like Groove Music Pass) you're currently signed up to.

Exploring the Maps App

Just like Google, Microsoft provides its own mapping service with the Maps app. This incredibly useful tool not only shows you a 2D map of anywhere in the world but also lets you see satellite view, traffic information and even view major cities in 3D. A new addition to Maps is the ability to draw or write on top of maps and save them for later.

Directions

You can use the Map app to plan routes: in a car, by public transport and even on foot. Select your chosen transportation method using the icons at the top of the Directions pane. You can either leave the A field as My Location or type a new one. In the B field, type your destination. The route will appear on the map. You can refine the route by clicking the options button.

Search

Click the search button on the left-hand side of the map window and a new pane will open. This pane contains some search suggestions, such as Hotels and Coffee and Shopping, with the standard search field at the top. As you type your search, suggestions will appear in the search pane. You can click any of these to find that location.

Maps View

The Maps view is the default one for the Maps app. This is what will greet you when you first load the app on your Windows 10 PC. You can zoom in and out of the map using either the + and – buttons on the control panel on the right of the window or by scrolling back and forward with the scroll wheel on your mouse (if you use one).

Your Location

When you open the Maps app it will try to pinpoint your approximate location. You may be asked to allow this location tracking to happen. Your location will then be show on the map as a small black and grey circle. You can click on this to see more information, if available, and then save the location as a favourite by clicking the star in the pane that opens.

Windows Ink

Windows Ink allows you to write or draw on a map using the various pen tools (including colours). You can also use the pen to trace a route and have Maps tell you the distance of the line drawn, or even the directions for the route you marked out. You can then save the customised map. It is really very clever and fun to play around with.

Maps Settings

The Maps app settings let you choose the units of measurement used, depending on your preference and your preferred defaults for directions and location. This last option will be used if the app can't find you, by using location services. You can also download maps for offline use or upload maps that have been saved elsewhere, that have been shared with you perhaps.

3D Cities

The 3D Cities button should be fairly self-explanatory. Click the button to open the pane and you will see an alphabetical list of the cities with thumbnails that have been mapped in 3D. Click the Country/Region heading at the top to refine the list. Click on any of the thumbnails to load the 3D map; loading time will vary, depending on your Internet connection speed.

Saved Places

The Saved Places pane contains all of your saved locations. These can be anything from a favourite coffee shop to the street where you parked your car in a new city. To add places, search for a location and select the star underneath the correct one in the search results list. You then have the option to give the favourite a nickname or set it as Home or Work.

Rotate & Tilt

The small floating control panel on the right of the Maps window contains several useful tools for changing the current view. The top two controls are rotate and tilt, allowing you to either rotate the map around the central point or tilt the map to give you an isometric view. You can easily centre your view on your location again by clicking the third icon down.

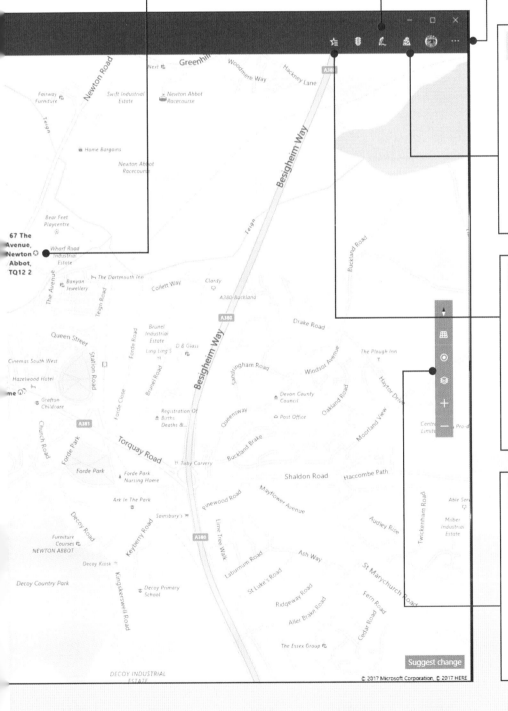

Navigating with the Maps App

Boasting excellent mapping, great aerial photography, up-to-the-minute traffic and the ability to calculate directions by public transport, road or foot, the Maps app is one of the very best ways to navigate. New additions make the Maps app even more useful, with new ways to get directions and plan routes added in the latest update.

Moving Around in Maps

There are few controls in the Maps app but they allow you to do a lot of things very easily. Let's take a look at how you move around in the app.

Step 1 The easiest way to move the map around is to left-click and drag it and use the mouse wheel or trackpad slider to zoom in and out. This allows you to move the map around to focus on the area you need. If you are zoomed far out of the map, double-clicking the mouse zooms in quickly.

Step 2 Maps has a dedicated control panel on the side of the window containing, from top to bottom: Rotate, hold pointer on it to see; Tilt, hold pointer over to see options; Show Location; Map Views/Layer; and Zoom in and Zoom out. You can also tilt by holding the right mouse button and moving up and down.

Step 3 Clicking on things like Saved Places or 3D Cities in the top control bar, tabs will line up alongside the permanent Search and Directions buttons at the top left of the window. You can then click on them at any time to see the information contained in each pane or tab.

Step 4 Right-clicking on the map brings up a small action menu. This lets you set a To location, a From location (for planning a route), add a new destination and drop a pin in a specific location. When you drop a pin, a new window opens allowing you to search for things at that location, add favourites and more.

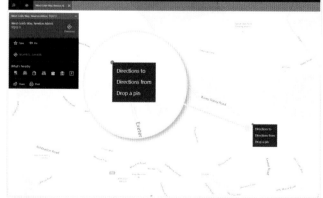

Planning a Route

Maps is great just for checking out an area, looking around a city or just finding businesses local to you. It is also great for planning detailed routes.

Step 1 To start planning a route, click the Directions tab at the top left of the Maps window. A small panel opens with boxes for your starting and ending location. You can either type a destination or you can choose one from the list that appears below the box when you click on it.

Step 2 If you need to make detours or multiple stops along your route, you can click the + button to add more destination boxes. Each one can have a destination in it, making up your complete route. When you view directions, each of the destinations you added is marked with a relevant letter.

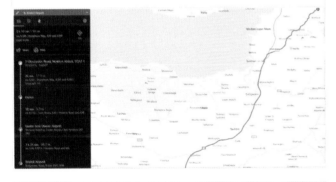

Step 3 Routes vary depending on whether you are driving, walking or need to take public transport. You can quickly flick between these options using the buttons at the top of the directions pane. When you have your start and end points entered and travel method chosen, click Get Directions.

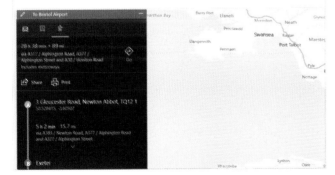

Step 4 The route is now shown on the map, with an estimated travel time readout above the destination. If alternative routes are available, they are shown as a light blue line, with the main route shown as a dark blue line. Points along the route are marked, usually where a change of direction is needed.

Step 5 If you click Go in the directions pane, Maps switches to a satnav-style view and traces your route as you continue along it. This is more for portable devices such as phones and tablets that you could use for directions in a vehicle. Click the Back button to return to the normal maps view.

Step 6 You can also plan a route by drawing it. Click the Ink button and then the Directions tool in the menu that opens. Draw a line along the route you wish to take and Maps refines that into a proper route along roads, missing dead-ends, etc. You can save or share the route just as with any other.

Using the People App

The People app has been a part of Windows 10 for some time but in the more recent update to the OS, it has had an overhaul. New features and options have been added, along with a brand new taskbar icon. Let's take a look at this excellent way of keeping track of your friends, family and other contacts.

The New People Button

If you can't see the People button in the taskbar, and can't activate it in the action menu, you may be running an older version of Windows 10. Check your available updates.

Step 1 After the newest Creators update has installed, you will see a small people icon on the right-hand side of the taskbar. If you don't see the icon (it looks like two people, one standing behind the other), right-click on the taskbar and select "Show the People Button" from the action menu.

Step 3 You may need to connect the apps before People will start checking for contacts. If an app is not already connected, but is available to be, it will have a link next to it: Click to connect this app. The app in question will open and it will be linked to People. Any new contacts in the app will be added.

Step 2 Click on the button and a new People panel will open. Click on the Get started button at the bottom of the new panel. Now click on the Apps tab. This will show you a list of apps that the People app is currently pulling contact information from. It may include apps such as Skype and Mail.

Step 4 The People tab in the panel will eventually show a list of regular contacts, or people you have Shoulder Tapped (or who have Shoulder Tapped you). Right now it will probably be empty and you can't manually add people to this panel; although this option may be added in the future.

Step 5   You can open the original (but updated) People app either through the People panel on the taskbar, or by clicking on it in the main apps list in the Start menu. To add a new contact manually to the People app, click on the People button, select the More button and then New Contact.

Step 6   The main app will open in a new window and you will be asked to choose and account to save the contact to: usually Outlook but can also include things like Gmail accounts, if you use one. You can then enter the name, phone number and any other contact details in the fields provided.

Step 7   You can add a photo to your contacts, just like on a smartphone, if you have one to hand. Click the Add photo circle on the new contact creation screen and navigate to the photo you want to use. The default photo selection is the Photos app but you can browser to any folder you want.

Step 8   The new People app allows you to pin a number of contacts to the right side of the taskbar for quick access. Click the People button and then click "Find and pin contacts". A list of your contacts will appear in the panel. Scroll down until you find the contact you want to pin.

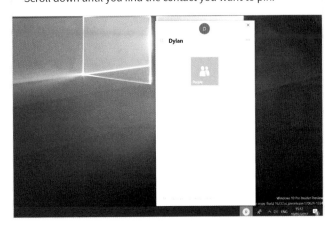

Step 9   Click on the contact to pin it to the taskbar. A separate window will also open, showing you the contact details. This is the windows that will open each time you click on a pinned contact. A well as the contact details, it also contains links to the main app, and options for unpinning.

Step 10   Shoulder Taps are notifications from contacts, from apps like Skype, that animate in the taskbar. To enable Shoulder Taps, go to Settings > Personalisation > Taskbar and scroll down to People. You can enable or disable Shoulder Taps and enable or disable Shoulder Tap sounds here.

Exploring the Calendar App

The Windows 10 Calendar app is a fully integrated planning tool, linked up to your email accounts and can easily be synced to your Windows Phone. Adding new events can be done manually or you can simply use it to view national and public holidays, all of which are automatically added based on your location.

New Event

There are two main ways to add a new event to your calendar. You can either click on the date in the main window or if the date you want is not in view, you can click the New Event button here. You can then add an event name, location and a start and end date. Give the event a short description, especially if you plan to share it with a contact. You can do that by adding people using the pane on the right of the Add Event screen.

Month Preview

No matter which view you choose for the main calendar pane - day, week, etc. - the month preview will always show a full month. You can use the arrows above the mini calendar to skip to different months and clicking on a date will then bring that date into view on the main calendar panel. The current day is highlighted in the Month Preview.

Linked Calendars

Your calendar can be linked to your email account, which will be shown here. If you are using Gmail for your email account, and have any calendars set up in Google Calendar, these will also be shown here. You can use the checkboxes to select and deselect calendars from showing in the main pane and each is colour coded, so you know which custom calendar an event comes from.

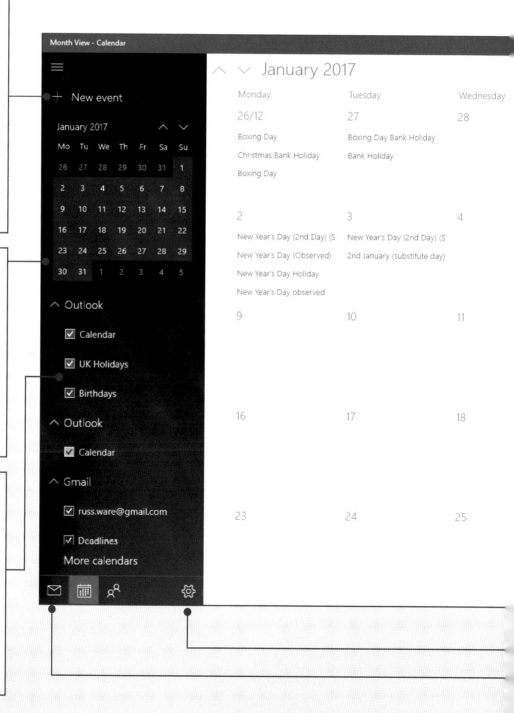

Calendar Pane

The main Calendar pane, however you choose to view it with the view buttons, contains a number of different bits of useful information. Public and national holidays are automatically added based on location. The current day is highlighted in your chosen highlight colour. The current day, along with a few days after, will also show weather and temperature information. Clicking the weather symbol will open the Weather app.

Calendar View

Along the top of the main window are the controls for changing how the calendar is viewed. The default is the full month view. You can switch to Day or multi-day using the dropdown menu and the calendar will be split into hourly sections. Work Week shows Monday to Friday only, letting you easily plan business or school commitments. To quickly return to the current day, click the Today button here.

Add Event

Click on any day in the main pane or any hourly slot in day view and a mini Add Event pane will open. You can use this to quickly add an event to your calendar. The pane includes event name, time slots and location; it also lets you choose which custom calendar to add it to. If you want to add more details, click the More Details button. If not, click Done to add the event.

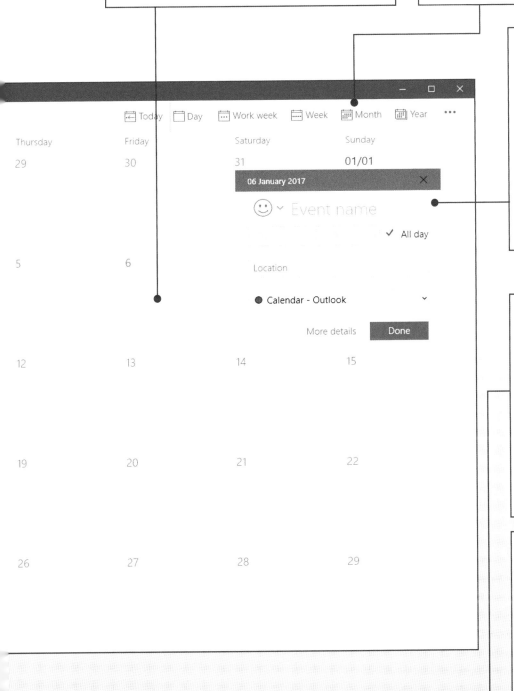

Calendar Settings

Alongside various customisation settings, such as the ability to choose light and dark themes and change the default highlight colour, are settings for adding new email accounts and changing the default view. You can also add public or national holidays manually, in Calendar Settings, if they have not been correctly added automatically. custom calendar an event comes from.

Switch to Mail

The Mail and Calendar apps are closely linked and you can quickly switch between the two using the buttons here. Receive an email with an appointment in it and you can quickly add it to your calendar using the tools in the Mail app. When you switch to the Mail app, it will open in a new window, so the Calendar can be viewed at the same time.

Plan Events and Appointments

Digital calendars are no longer the preserve of business people scheduling appointments via email. With mobile phones now our new diaries, digital calendars are being used by increasing numbers of people to organise their busy lives. Welcome to Calendar.

Schedule Appointments and More

If used properly, and particularly if synced to a Windows phone, the calendar can be a great tool. We'll show you how to set up your calendar, arrange events and change settings so your calendar is exactly the way you want it.

Multiple Calendars The best thing about the Windows 10 Calendar app is how admirably it copes with multiple calendars. So providing they invite your account, you're able to easily see calendars from friends and relatives. It's also easy to schedule your own events, of course.

Sign In Now add the accounts you want to incorporate into Calendar. You can come back and do this at any point you choose via Settings > Accounts. From there you can easily add an Outlook.com, Exchange, Google or iCloud calendar or enter advanced settings for any other calendars you may have from other providers.

Different Accounts Like Windows 10's Email app, Calendar also enables you to add multiple accounts and from different providers, too. So whether you use an Outlook calendar at work or have shared Google calendars, you can join them all together in the Calendar app. First click on Add Accounts.

Allow Location Next, you'll be asked to enable location access for Mail and Calendar. This is predominantly for one very simple reason – Calendar shows you the weather for your location each day. You can always revoke access via the Settings app. Go to Location and you can turn off Calendar's access to Location. You can always turn off location permanently there, too.

Your Calendar

This is our calendar. Notice that this week has the weather showing – a nice touch if you enabled location in the previous step. Notice that we've only got one calendar at the moment on the left. If we had multiple calendars from different providers, these would show here and you could turn them on and off.

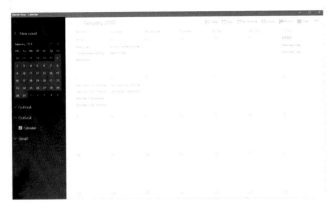

New Event

Click the New Event button in the top left and you'll see a screen that looks very much like this. Add the name of the event, a location should you wish to, plus start and end dates and times. You're also able to invite people by email using the field on the right-hand side. This will then insert the event into their calendar as well.

Repeat Events

You can also choose to repeat events – just click the Repeat button in the toolbar when you're creating a new event. Here you'll see we're creating a recurring event for our trips to the gym. Check the days you want. You can repeat daily, weekly, monthly or yearly depending on what you need to do.

Weekly View

Here's our thrice-weekly gym event in our calendar. This is a weekly calendar view (we were on the monthly one in our previous steps); you can change the view in the top right. You can also go forward or back through the weeks using the arrows – also in the top right.

Change Settings

The cog icon in the bottom left takes you to your Calendar Settings menu. Here you can do things like edit settings for extra accounts, but you can also change the calendar to suit the way you work – which days are in your work week, for example, and which day do you consider to be the first of the week?

Calendar Colours

You're able to assign different colours to different calendar accounts. Note that our Outlook.com account has also synchronised two more calendars from our online account – UK Holidays and our Birthday calendar – and that we've given these different colours so they show up better in the main calendar view.

Exploring the Photos App

You can use the Photos app to view or edit photos and videos in your Pictures library and on OneDrive, and to import photos and videos. The Photos app includes a wide range of editing options to enhance your photos, from automatic fixes to advanced adjustments.

Sort by Date

Whilst in the Collection section, you can quickly find photos from a certain time period without scrolling through all of the ones in the full list. Above each collection you will see a date; click or tap on the date to zoom out to a list of all past months. Click a month to zoom in on that date.

Photos Menu

The new photos app has two main internal sections: Collection and Albums. Alongside these sections are Folders, which show other images on your computer. In the Collection section, you'll see a collection of all your photos, grouped by date taken (in reverse chronological order).

Photo Collection

All photos within a particular collection are shown here; you can select images by rolling over them with the mouse pointer and checking the boxes which appear in the top corner of each image. Click on any image thumbnail shown on the main screen and it will open in full screen mode.

Photo Albums

The Photos app will automatically create some albums for you, based on images which share characteristics (such as screenshots) but you can also create your own albums. Click the New Album button and all of your images are shown. Select the ones you want to add and click the tick.

PHOTOS SETTINGS

The Photos settings mainly consist of ways to change how the Auto Enhance and linked duplicate options work. There are, however, a few other settings worth looking at. You can change or add image sources and allow content stored in OneDrive to be included in the app.

Image Editing

The image editing screen introduces a range of different editing tools. The left-hand menu shows the main tool sections (Basic Fixes, Filters, etc.) and the tools within those sections appear on the right of the image. You can zoom the image by rolling over it and clicking the + button.

Contextual Menu

With no image selected, the button in the top right corner of the photos app allows you to refresh the view, change to selection mode (for selecting multiple images) or import photos. Once a photo is selected, these buttons change to Share, Copy and Delete image.

Full Screen Mode

Once an image in the Photos app is viewed in full screen, you have access to several new tools. Along the top of the image are buttons to Share, create a Slideshow, Enhance, Edit, Rotate and Delete the image. You can return to the thumbnail view by clicking the Back button.

Auto Enhance

If you don't want to mess around with image editing, you can try out the Auto Enhance button. Clicking this button once will allow the Photo app software to analyse the image and apply changes. This might simply be enhancing the brightness or colour and it could straighten the image as well.

Importing Photos to Your PC

Importing your photos from a digital camera or phone on to your PC may seem like a very simple task to some but if you have never done it before, you can encounter problems and have no idea how to get around them. Here we take a look at importing photos from phone, tablet or camera, using a standard USB cable and tools already included in Windows 10.

Importing to a Folder

Importing your photos or images directly to a folder on the desktop, or elsewhere, is the traditional method. It tends to be quicker but offers fewer importing options.

Step 1 The first thing you need to do to import photos directly from a phone or camera is to connect the relevant cable to your PC. In almost all cases, this will be a USB cable of some sort. You will have been supplied a transfer cable with the device you are using. Plug this into a free USB port.

Step 2 Plug the other end in to your phone or digital camera and wait a few moments. Your PC should detect the device and may need to install some drivers to make the USB connection work.

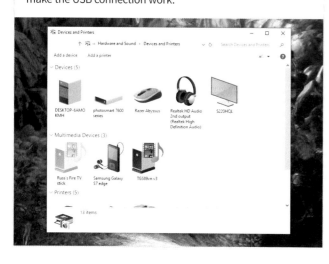

Step 3 Normally, when you first plug a device in to your computer which contains storage of some sort, Windows will ask how you want to handle the files in that storage. Scroll own the list to see 'Open in a Folder'. In some cases, Explorer will open showing the connected device.

Step 4 Now click on the device storage: this may be Phone and Card on a smartphone and navigate to where the photos are stored. This will normally be in a folder called DCIM on your phone or camera. You can now simply cut and paste or drag and drop images to a new folder on your PC.

Importing to the Photos App

The Windows 10 Photos app is a great tool for importing photos from a phone, tablet or camera. It allows you to preview and individually pick images more easily, and even sorts them.

Step 1 Open the Photos app on your Windows 10 PC. Now connect your phone or camera to your computer using the relevant USB cable. If you see the popup menu asking how you want to deal with the storage media you just connected, ignore it or click it closed.

Step 2 The Photos app should have opened up with the Collections screen showing. If not, click the tab at the top to open it now. Along the top of the Collections tab are your controls: Refresh, Select, Slideshow and Import. Import is the only one you need to click at this point.

Step 3 The Photos app will now search for photos available to be imported. If your device is not connected properly, or the correct USB drivers are not installed, it will fail to find anything at this point. If you are transferring from a phone or tablet, you may also have to unlock the screen to continue.

Step 4 By default, every image detected on your device will be selected for importing. If you want to import everything, click Continue. If not, you can use the check boxes on the images to select those you want to import; use the Clear All and Select All buttons as required.

Step 5 You can now choose where the imported photos will be saved. By default, this will probably be somewhere like **C:\Users\YourName\Pictures**. Click the 'Change where they're imported' link to do just that. You can also choose to import into folders arranged by month or day.

Step 6 Click Import. Your image will now begin to appear in the Photos app window, within the Collections section. An album will also be created called Last Import. Click on one of the images shown to begin editing or enhancing it with the tools Photos offers.

Using the Photos App

The integrated Photos app was first introduced in Windows 8 but it wasn't the best experience when compared to most third party apps. In Windows 10 and again in the Anniversary update it has been much improved, with better ways to browse photos and a lot more editing options and controls to make the most of the images on your PC.

Managing Your Images

The Photos app has seen some useful improvements over the last few years and is actually very powerful now. It doesn't offer the flexibility of an app like Photoshop Elements, but it does a lot of simple edits very well.

Step 1 Photos shows all of your images in a scrolling timeline of images, like we're now used to seeing on many smartphones or tablets. This is called your photos Collection. You can click on any image to get a full-window view and then click the Back arrow in the top left corner to return to the main list.

Step 2 Albums is a completely automated feature. If you have an iPhone or iPad, you may have seen Apple's Moments feature; this works in much the same way. Albums gathers together groups of photos you took around the same time, so you can easily look back through them later.

Step 3 If you're signed into Windows 10 with your Microsoft account, you'll also be signed in automatically to the Photos app. The benefit of this is that photos stored on OneDrive also appear in Photos. You can auto-upload photos from the OneDrive app for your phone as you take them.

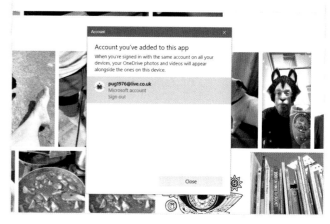

Step 4 Photos settings, click the More button at the top right, lets you choose whether the Photos app atomically enhances badly exposed photos as well as whether you want the app to show duplicate images as one file; say you saved a photo twice or imported it twice without realising.

Step 5 You can also choose where Photos should look for images here. Your own Pictures folder, plus Windows' public Photos folder are automatically included; but it's really useful to be able to change this if you store your images somewhere else, perhaps an external hard drive you always use.

Step 6 Back to the Photos Collection. You're now going to use the Select feature, found in the menu at the top right. This enables you to select individual or multiple images. You'll see the top menu bar has now changed, while each image has a tick box appear on it. Click it to choose the images you want.

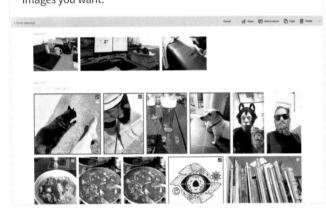

Step 7 The Photos app allows you to do several things with your photos and images. The first is to email them. Select the images you want to send and click the Share button in the toolbar. The share options window will open, allowing you to choose how to share the images, including Mail.

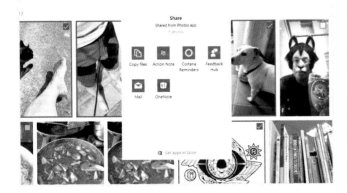

Step 8 You can also copy your photos and images into another app or File Explorer window. To do this, select the photos you want, then click the Copy button in the toolbar (the old Ctrl-C keyboard shortcut works too). You can then paste the photos wherever you want on your computer.

Step 9 To delete photos, select them as detailed previously and click the Delete button in the Toolbar. You will see a pop-up to confirm you want to continue with the action. Deleted photos are moved to the recycle bin anyway, so you have a chance to retrieve photos deleted in error.

Step 10 The final tool in the Select toolbar is the Add to Album button. This adds any images you have selected to either one of the auto-created albums, or to an album you create for the purpose. Click 'Create new album' in the popup window, give it a name and then click 'Create album'.

Drawing on Images

The Photos app in Windows 10 allows you to draw or write on top of your images, as long as you have installed the Anniversary update, and then save them as a completely new file.

Step 1 Open the Photos app and select your image (or double click an image to open it in Photos if that is the default app). Along the top of the image are several buttons, click the Draw button to begin editing your image. You will see a new set of buttons and controls appear at the top.

Step 2 From left to right, these buttons allow you to draw/write in pen style, pencil style, calligraphy style, erase, switch out of touch writing mode, save your file, share your file, and exit drawing mode. If you click on any button and see a small arrow, click again to open a contextual menu for it.

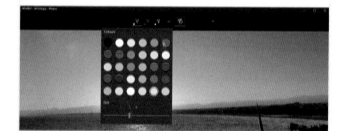

Step 3 The contextual menus allow you to change the colour and the thickness of the pen or pencil tools. When you have picked a style, colour and size, you can begin to draw or write over the top of your image. The drawing tool in Photos works best with a touchscreen PC, of course.

Step 4 Once you have completed drawing or writing on your image, you can save it. If you want to retain the original image, change the name of the edited image in the save dialogue box before you finish. If you click on Share, a list of sharing possibilities will appear to choose from.

Editing Images

The image editing tools in the Photos app have been improved and added to in the Anniversary update, including the addition of preset filters and effects.

Step 1 Open your image in Photos and click on the Edit button at the top right of the screen. If you had the Photos app running in full screen, the image will be shrunk down slightly to fit the new toolbar, down the right of the of the editing window.

Step 2 Starting at the top of the editing toolbar, you have the crop and rotate button. Click this to see further options for managing the aspect of your image. You can choose a preset aspect ratio, or drag the handles at the corners to crop to a custom shape.

Step 3 If you need to straighten the image, you can do so using the handle to the right of the photo. Click on this and move your mouse up or down to carefully rotate the image in small amounts. As you do this, a grid appears to help you line up the photo. Click Finished when done.

Step 6 The tools in the Adjust tab allow you to tweak the Light, Colour, Warmth and Clarity of an image. You can also use a slider to apply a Vignette (lighten or darken the edges of an image). Just use the sliders to adjust any of these effects until you are happy with your image.

Step 4 Moving down the main edit toolbar you will see the Enhance button. You can click this to let the software make changes and improvements to the image automatically. You will see the image change slightly, and you can then use the slider on the button to increase or decrease those changes.

Step 7 At the bottom of the Adjust tab are Spot Fix and Red Eye tools. Click Spot Fix and the cursor will change to a blue circle. Place this over the part of the image you want to fix and click. The software will try to match the location of dot to the scenery or colour around it, hopefully removing it.

Step 5 You can, of course, apply enhancements yourself. Below the auto-enhance button are the photo filters. Click on any of these to see the changes applied to your image. You can apply a filter and then adjust its effects by clicking on the Adjust tab at the top of the toolbar.

Step 8 The Red Eye tool works in a similar way. Click the tool and move the circle cursor over the red part of your subject's eye and zoom in if you need to. The tool will try to take the red out of the image and match it to the surrounding colour. The results are usually very good.

Exploring the Groove Music App

The Groove Music app has been continually updated since the launch of Windows 10 and is now a fully featured music player and music discovery app. If you have not looked at the app for a while, you should take a look now and check out the additions and changes that have been made. Groove Music is now the only app you need for listening to music on your PC.

Music Search

You can use the music search bar to quickly find specific tracks or albums on your computer. As you search, suggestions will appear below the search box. When results are shown, you can play the song or album directly from the results. You can also search on the Music Store for the same term.

Music Store

The Music Store can be accessed directly from the Groove Music app. For a low monthly fee, Groove Music Pass lets you stream and download music from one of the biggest music catalogues on the planet. Custom radio stations play hours of music based on your favourite artists too.

Groove Radio

Once you have a Groove Music account, a new option, Groove Radio, will appear in the music menu. As with other platforms' music services, you can start a radio station for music similar to an artist, song or album you select. Once you start a station, the related music plays.

New Playlist

You can create a playlist of any music currently on your computer. Click the New Playlist button and give your playlist a name. This will then be listed under the New Playlist button. To add a song to your playlist, right-click on it and select Add to and choose your playlist.

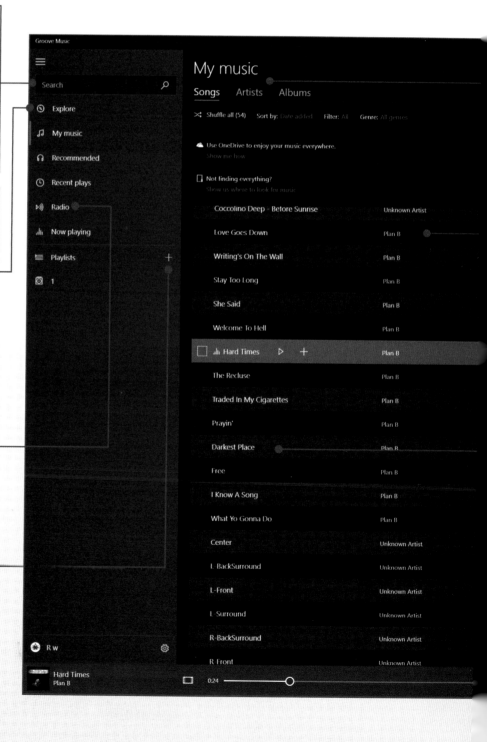

GROOVE MUSIC SETTINGS

Along with options for setting up a Groove Music Pass, and some basic customisation options, the Groove Music settings allow you to change where it looks for music on your computer and also lets you import iTunes playlists in a few simple steps.

Music Menu

Your music collection is organised into sections, including Artist, Album and Songs. You can view your collection via any of these listings by clicking the links. The Now Playing option, as the name suggests, shows you the current song or album in the music player.

Track Listing

All of the music in a particular category, Albums, Artists, etc., is shown on the main screen when the category is selected. You can filter the listed music and change how the list is displayed using the controls along the top of the list. Double-click any song to start it playing.

Pinning Music

The Groove Music app lets you pin specific playlists or albums to the Start menu, making it quicker and easier to play your favourite music. To pin an album or playlist, search or navigate to one and then right-click on its name. From the action menu, select Pin to Start.

Music Controls

When a song is selected in the track listing screen, the Music Controls along the bottom of the screen become usable. As well as a progress bar, there are buttons for skip forward/backward, play, volume, shuffle and repeat. The title of the currently playing song will also be displayed.

Using Groove Music

When Windows 10 first launched, the Groove Music app seemed to be a bit of an afterthought. It wasn't an exciting music player and the online song library wasn't that great compared to other music stores. However, recent updates and a push to build the music store means that Groove music is now a definite player when it comes to listening to tunes.

Listening to Music

First we will look at how you listen to music you have on your computer already, including how you use Groove Music to find your music files.

Step 1 Open the Groove Music app and click on My music in the left sidebar. The app should have automatically scanned your computer for any compatible music files (MP3 etc.) and will display them as a list. You can change how the music is displayed by clicking the Song, Artist or Album tabs.

Step 2 If you think that music you have on your computer isn't being shown, you can direct Groove Music to look in specific folders or locations on your computer. Click the 'Show us where to look for music' link just below the tabs at the top. Click the + button and navigate to the folder your files are in.

Step 3 By default, the Music folder of your PC will be selected but you can add as many folders as you like, including Downloads and OneDrive. When you have added all the possible music folders on your computer, click the Done button and hopefully you will see all of your music listed.

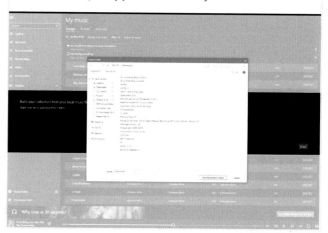

Step 4 To play a single song, click the Songs tab and find the song in the list. Move your mouse over it and click the play button that appears; you can also right-click on a song and select play from the menu that appears. The song currently playing will be shown at the bottom, with the controls.

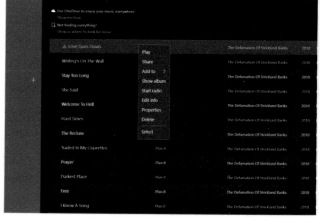

Step 5 The controls will always be displayed at the bottom of the app and include the standard music player controls of Previous (song), Pause, Next (song), Shuffle, Repeat and a volume controller. You can also drag the progress slider to skip forwards or backwards within a song that's playing.

Step 6 You can create your own playlists from all of the songs available quite easily. Move the mouse over a song and click the + button instead of play. Click 'New playlist' and give it a name and then 'Create playlist'. Move over the next song you want to add, click the + button and add it to your new list.

Buying New Music

Groove Music lets you buy and listen to music from a huge online library as well as being a music player app. You will need a Groove Music Pass to download songs or albums.

Step 1 Open Groove Music and click Explore in the sidebar. You can then search for songs or albums or just browse through the various categories to find something you like. You can listen to a 30 second sample of any song but if you want to download it and listen to it all, you will need a pass.

Step 3 Find a song or album you want and select it. You can then either right-click on individual tracks and select Download or you can click the download button at the top of the album screen to download the whole thing. Once downloaded, songs or albums will appear in the My music list.

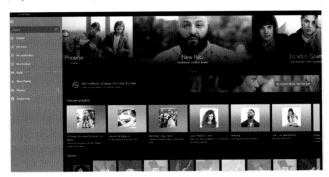

Step 2 There will almost certainly be a free trial pass on offer, so take advantage of this to see if you will get value from paying the normal monthly fee (around £9/$9). Click 'Try Groove Music pass for free' and follow the instructions to set up an account. Once done, you can begin downloading music.

Step 4 Another way to listen to music you don't have on your computer is to use the Radio feature of Groove music. Click Radio in the sidebar and browse or search for a station you want to listen to. You will need to be signed in to your Groove Music account to listen to the radio stations.

Using the Phone Companion

The Phone Companion app allows you to connect and sync your phone to your Windows 10 computer more easily. With a Windows phone, there's nothing extra needed. But for an Android phone or iPhone, to make it work seamlessly in conjunction with your Windows 10 PC, you need to follow a few steps to get the right apps on your phone.

Setting Up Phone Companion

Before you get started, you will need to make sure that you're logged into your machine using a verified Microsoft Live account, and that you have your Android or iOS device on hand.

Step 1 If, for some reason, you do not already have Phone Companion installed on your Windows 10 PC, you can download it from the Store for free. To open Phone Companion, click the Start button and then select Phone Companion from the apps list; or type phone companion in the search box.

Step 2 When you run Phone Companion for the first time, you see a simple screen with the top three mobile operating systems. To get started, click your desired mobile OS. In this example, we are using Android but the process is almost identical for iOS. Windows phones have slightly more features available.

Step 3 Connect the device to your PC using a USB data cable (the charging cable that came with your phone). After a few seconds when the phone connects to the computer, a hidden tab will appear at the bottom of the Phone Companion window labelled Show.

Step 4 If you click on the Show link at the bottom of the screen, it reveals more details about your device, such as the amount of storage used, with links to import photos, videos and files using File Explorer. If you are using a Windows phone, you will also see additional info, such as battery life remaining.

Step 5 If you choose to import videos and photos from the device, they will be placed in the Windows 10 HYPERLINK "https://www.groovypost.com/howto/print-windows-10-photos-universal-apps/" Photos app, which means they will automatically sync with OneDrive. If you don't want to do that, you can browse the device and copy over your photos and videos manually.

Looking for new photos and videos

0 items found so far

Cancel

Step 6 The other useful feature of the Phone Companion is the ability to discover and quickly add key Microsoft apps for your mobile device. The apps available for Android and iOS include Cortana, OneDrive, OneNote, Skype, Office (Word, Excel and PowerPoint) and Outlook.

Work from wherever, your files are synced
Step 1 of 4

Get each Office app for Android – they're free

Everything you need to get it done when you're on your phone or tablet. And when you're back at your PC, your files are automatically up to date.

Choose one to get started

- Word
- Excel
- PowerPoint

Step 7 Click on the Get Started button below the app you want to add or set up. You will see a link to download the app from the Play Store or App Store; or you can enter your email address and get a download link sent to your inbox, allowing you to add it at a later date.

Take Cortana with you on your phone and tablet
Step 1 of 3

Get Cortana on your Android phone or tablet – it's free

Cortana reminds you about the things you need to do, even when you're away from your PC.

Download it for your phone or tablet from Google Play, or email yourself a link. Use an email address that you can easily check on your phone or tablet:

| Email address | Send |

While the app is downloading, go to the next step.

Step 8 For Phone Companion to work properly with things like the Cortana app, you will need to make sure that you sign in to the app on your phone using the same Microsoft account you use on your computer.

You're signed into this PC with this Microsoft account

 Russell Ware

To sync your stuff automatically, you need to use the same Microsoft account on your phone or tablet, too.

Not you?

OFFICE ON ANDROID

The Microsoft Office Mobile apps have the familiar look and feel of Office with an intuitive touch experience designed for Android phones and tablets. They are completely free to use on Android, allowing you to view, edit and create documents on the go; and get quick access to your files in the cloud whenever you need them. Your Office documents maintain the same formatting across your PC and mobile devices and you can easily share your documents with others by just emailing an attachment or a hyperlink. You can install the Microsoft apps using the Phone Companion app for Windows 10, which is explained above, or you can simply go into the Play Store and search for the apps you want.

Using Skype in Windows 10

Now that Microsoft owns Skype it has tried to incorporate it into Windows 10 but rules on being anti-competitive seem to have prevented it from bundling the chat and video call service with the OS. However, you get a Windows app that's basically an invitation to download the full version as we shall explain.

Install and Use Skype

Recently updated, Skype has now been turned into a proper Windows 10 app and follows the Windows design style more closely.

Step 1 Skype has a dedicated Windows 10 app and this may be preinstalled on your Windows PC but you might need to download it from the Windows store. You can also download Skype directly from "http://www.skype.com" www.skype.com as well as check that you have the latest version available.

Step 2 Once installed, you will need to sign in to the Skype app. If you already have a Skype account, which is completely free to set up, just enter your login details when prompted. If not, you can go to www.login.skype.com and create a new account in just a few minutes.

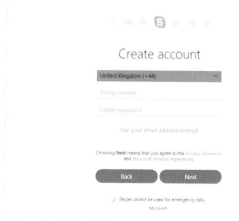

Step 3 The Skype window should now be open on screen. The default view is the Recent conversations screen but this may be completely empty if you are new to Skype. The first thing you need to do as a fresh user, is to begin adding contacts.

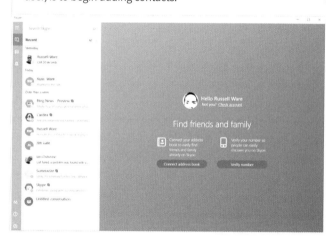

Step 4 Click the Contacts button (2nd button down from the top) and either select the add contact icon at the bottom of the sidebar or click directly in the search text box and type the name, Skype name or email of the person you want to add. Click Search Skype.

Step 5 Select your friend from the search results, assuming you can see them in the list, and click Add to Contacts. Type a quick note to introduce yourself and then click Send. They will receive a request from you, along with the message and can choose whether to accept you or not.

Step 6 You can select any contact from your contacts list and then either instant message them or start a voice or video call. If the contact you click on has Skype, the call option buttons will appear in the top right corner of the window. Click the relevant button to start a call.

Step 7 Skype instant messaging makes it easy to keep in touch with your contacts and groups wherever they are. You can share files, photos and contacts. To instant message one of your contacts, select their name and start typing at the bottom of the main window.

Step 8 If you want to make calls to contacts not using Skype (you can make calls to mobiles and landlines too), you will need to add some Skype credit. To do this, click on your profile picture in the bottom left and click the 'Add Skype credit' link.

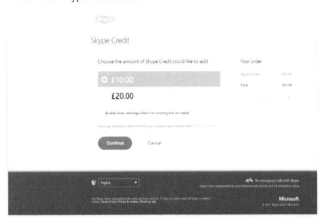

Step 9 Skype also now includes Bots. Bots are artificially intelligent programs that can do many useful things like search for news, summarise webpages, play games and more. You can start chatting with a bot just like you chat with friends, just choose a bot and click Get started.

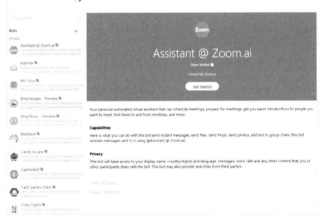

Step 10 Bots vary in how useful they are but some are well worth taking a look at. Take the Bing News bot for example. Add this and then type a word ("Crime" for example) in the conversation window. The bot will return news stories based on that subject.

Using Windows 10 Maintenance Tools

Before you start to add software to help with PC and Windows 10 maintenance, it is worth checking out the numerous tools included with the OS. These are slightly spread out over several different settings menus and tool folders but once you know where to find them, you will see that they can really help with system security and performance.

Maintaining Windows 10

Windows 10 is a lot better at keeping you informed of problems than previous versions were. It is, however, up to you to keep on top on maintaining the OS if you want the best experience.

Storage Sense Activating Storage Sense lets the system software automatically free up storage space by getting rid of files you no longer need. These can include temporary files such as cookies and the contents of your Recycle Bin.

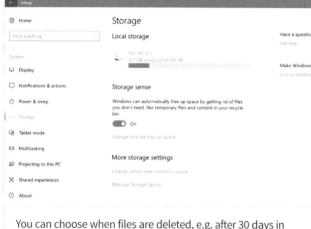

You can choose when files are deleted, e.g. after 30 days in the Recycle Bin or if apps don't use them for a certain amount of time. Alternatively you can simply click a button to Clean Now rather than setting automatic cleaning. You can find the Storage Sense option in Settings > System > Storage.

Background Apps One of the easiest ways to conserve power (for laptop users) and reduce processor strain, is to take control of Background Apps. These are apps that are, by default, allowed to receive info, send notifications and update in the background.

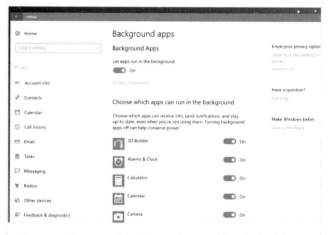

You can either stop all background apps with a single slider click or you can prevent individual apps from running in the background. Go to Settings > Privacy > Background Apps and look through the apps listed. If you see apps that you don't need notifications or updates from, click the slider to disable its background activity.

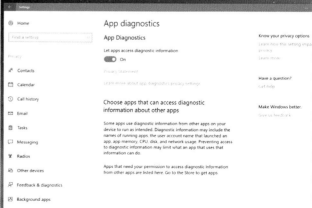

Troubleshooters

Windows 10 includes a number of troubleshooting tools, aimed specifically at certain problems such as audio loss or patchy Internet connection. This is often the best place to start when trying to solve problems with your PC and Windows 10, as the OS contains many drivers for common devices and may just need a small software update.

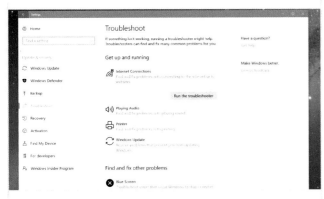

You simply look through the list of troubleshooters and click on the one which applies. Choose Run the Troubleshooter and then follow the instructions to try and solve the problem. You can find the troubleshooters in Settings > Update & Security > Troubleshoot.

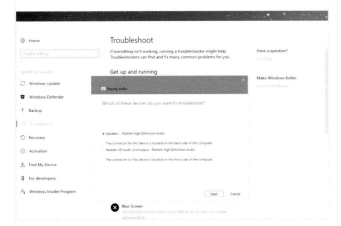

Disk Management

The Disk Management tool is more about diagnostics than actual maintenance but it is a useful way of checking whether your hard disk has space available and is healthy. The panel will show all of your disks, as well as all of the partitions.

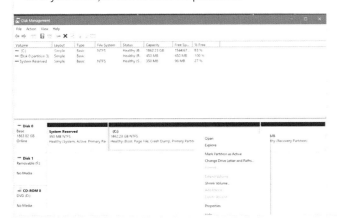

Disk Tools

There are several tools built in to Windows 10 (and also in older versions of the OS) that allow you to clean, fix and manage your hard disk. Open the File Explorer and look in the left-hand column for 'This PC'. Select it and then right click on Local Disk (C:). In the General tab, you will see a button for Disk Clean-up that lets you get rid of temporary Internet files, old program files and so on.

If you click the Tools tab, you can use the Error Checking tool and the Disk Defragment tool. Both of these tools can help your hard disk run more efficiently. Click on either button and follow the instructions for each.

Each column contains information about capacity, free space in MB, percentage of free space and health status. There are some further options, such as the ability to change drive letters and mark partitions as active but they are probably not worth playing around with unless you know what you are doing.

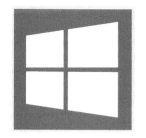

Exploring the Task Manager

The Task Manager is a very useful tool but even if you have been using Windows for some time, you might never have looked at it before. The Task Manager contains information on PC performance, the number of running apps, how many processes are pulling power from the processor and much more.

Processes Tab

The Processes tab is the default tab when the Task Manager is opened. You can open the task manager by simply searching for it in the main search panel. Just as with any other app or piece of software in Windows 10, you can pin a shortcut to the Task Manager, to the taskbar or as a desktop icon.

Process List

With the Processes tab selected, a list of all processes is shown. Processes are bits of software that run in the background, either running or waiting to run when a corresponding action is taken. As you can see from the list here, things like Cortana and AVG are shown; these you would obviously want to leave.

Resource Usage

If you find your PC becoming slow and sluggish during normal use, you may have too many processes running. By looking at the resource usage chart, you can see exactly which apps are taking up the most processing power, physical memory, disk space and even network bandwidth. If something is particularly resource hungry, you can right-click and stop it.

	Task Manager		
File Options View			
Processes Performance App history Startup Users Details Services			
		6%	34%
Name		CPU	Memory
Apps (9)			
Google Chrome		0%	109.4 MB
Free stock photos of eye conta...			
Microsoft Edge		0%	15.0 MB
Sticky Notes		0%	25.6 MB
Store		0%	58.8 MB
Task Manager		3.1%	15.0 MB
Thunderbird (32 bit)		0%	270.6 MB
Inbox - russ@bdmpublications...			
Windows Explorer (3)		0.1%	159.4 MB
Pictures			
Radeon ReLive			
Saved Pictures			
WPS Spreadsheets (32 bit)		0%	86.9 MB
Windows 10 Guidebook 20 - F...			
WPS Writer (32 bit)		0.1%	127.8 MB
Seniors 19 amends - v1.doc - ...			
Background processes (67)			
AMD External Events Service M...		0%	1.0 MB
AMD External Events Utility			
AMD ReLive: Desktop Overlay		0%	2.2 MB
AMD ReLive: Host Application		0%	1.8 MB
Application Frame Host		0%	10.1 MB
AVG Antivirus (32 bit)		0%	7.8 MB
AVG Service (32 bit)		0%	26.2 MB
AVG Service Process		0%	10.4 MB
AVG Software Analyzer		0%	71.5 MB
AVG User Interface (32 bit)		0%	6.3 MB
Avira (32 bit)		0%	2.4 MB
Avira Service Host (32 bit)		0%	2.0 MB
Bonjour Service (32 bit)		0%	1.3 MB
Browser_Broker		0%	2.9 MB
CCleaner		0%	5.2 MB
COM Surrogate		0%	2.0 MB
Cortana		0%	37.0 MB
Device Association Framework ...		0%	5.9 MB
Dual Controller (32 bit)		0%	3.5 MB
Elevation Proxy		0%	8.0 MB
Fewer details			

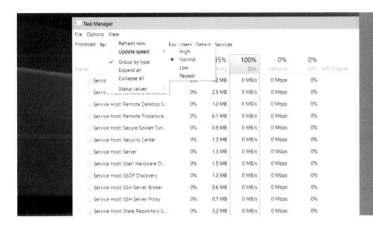

VIEW OPTIONS

The View options at the top of the Task Manager window allows you to do several things. You can manually refresh the current tab and also change the automatic update speed. For example you can change how the processes are displayed. Either by grouping them by type, expanding or collapsing the list, or showing status values.

Start-up Tab

The Start-up tab contains a list of all the apps, programs and processes that are enabled every time you start your computer. If your computer is brand new, this list should be fairly small and filled with essential items. But as you install new apps and software, this start-up list can become bloated and slow down boot up. You can disable auto start-up here.

Performance Tab

Another useful tab in the Task Manager is Performance. This gives you a real-time performance overview, allowing you to pinpoint exactly how well your hardware is coping with whatever you are doing at the time. If Task Manager is the only app open, the performance chart should be very stable but if you are running several apps, it will show any power spikes.

Fewer Details

You can view a limited version of the Task Manager by clicking on the "Fewer Details" button at the bottom of the window. This makes the window small enough that it can be left open, in the corner of your desktop for example, but still show relevant information. You can get more information at any time by clicking "More Details".

Free Up Storage Space

Disk Clean-up is the best way to free up space on your PC. It will clear up redundant files accumulating on your hard drive including temporary files and Downloaded Program files. But that's not the only way you can free up space, as you'll see…

Clearing Space on Your PC

It's worth giving your machine a little spring clean every so often to keep it lean. And that doesn't just mean removing unwanted files and folders from the desktop. Disk Clean-up should be an essential part of your PC maintenance.

Clean Up Disk Clean-up is a utility included with every copy of Windows. When you launch it (here we've searched for it using the search box on the taskbar), you'll get this small window appear. It will help you rid your PC of detritus that builds up over time as you download files from the Internet or install and uninstall apps.

Scan Results If you're scanning a second hard drive, it's unlikely Disk Clean-up will find a lot on it as it is mostly concerned with Windows files. And that's what we're looking at here in the results window. As you can see, you can check which items you want to remove from your PC. Click OK to remove.

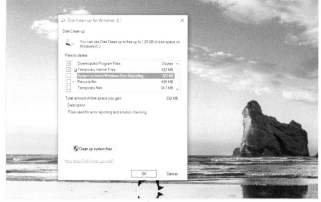

Which Drive? You'll be asked to select the drive you want to clean up. Most of the time there'll only be one drive you wish to clean up (your C: drive), but it could well be that you've got more than one storage drive on your PC. Disk Clean-up will then begin to scan your drive for things it can sweep up.

System Files We actually didn't click OK in the last step; instead clicking the Clean Up System Files option. This won't harm your Windows installation, but will clean up extraneous files that some people prefer to keep. If you upgraded from an old copy of Windows, this includes your Windows.old folder on your hard drive.

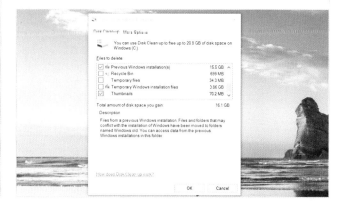

More Options

If you click the More Options tab, you'll see this window, taking you straight to the Add/Remove Programs area of Control Panel. It also gives you the option to remove old restore points that take up space inside Windows. The latest restore point will always be kept in case of a problem with your PC.

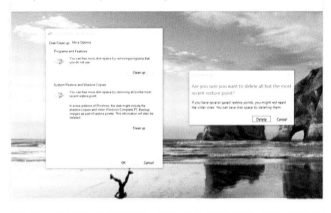

Uninstaller

Each desktop app has a different type of installer (or, in this case, uninstaller). Many are very similar, but you do get ones that differ, and one such is this app from Microsoft. Often you will be asked if you want to repair the application. You don't – you want to uninstall.

Programs and Features

This area of Control Panel is one of the most used, although it's not designed to be utilised quite as much in Windows 10 – the idea is that you'd uninstall using the method in the final step on this page. Still, it's the only way to see how much space your desktop applications are taking up. You can also access it via Control Panel > Programs.

Windows Features

This is for advanced users only. Also from this screen you can select Turn Windows Features On or Off. You're able to uninstall elements of Windows that you don't use – perhaps the old Internet Explorer, for example, or Microsoft's Print to PDF plug-in if you have an alternative solution that you use.

Other Users

If you try and uninstall a program with other users logged onto the PC, you'll always get a warning that other people may be using the application and so it may not uninstall properly. Get other users to log off before uninstalling programs if this is an issue.

Uninstall from Start

You're also able to easily uninstall apps from the Start menu – simply right-click on the app in question and select Uninstall from the menu that appears. It's the best way to uninstall any app, whether it's come from the Windows Store or not.

10 Tips to Speed Up Windows 10

There are many ways to improve the performance of your PC. Some will produce only marginal improvements and some only speed up operations such as web searches; but when you're trying to squeeze the most out of your system every little helps. Here are some handy tips to boost the performance of almost any Windows 10 system, but particularly those that are a few years old.

Performance without Pain

Gaining improvements in performance is pointless if it means you need to spend 3 hours a day running cleaner software or rooting through old files. These tips will improve performance, without the pain.

Install the Latest Windows Updates

Microsoft normally releases updates monthly, although important updates will be released as needed. You should check for and install available Windows Updates, which could include: bug fixes, security patches, Windows Defender malware definitions, etc., that could help keep your system stable and improve the performance of Windows.

Switch to a Faster DNS Server

If your ISP doesn't maintain its Domain Name Server (DNS) properly it will slow down your web searches and make connecting to websites slow and unreliable. Slow and poorly maintained DNS servers are one of the main causes of problems connecting to websites. Consider adding or using a fast DNS server like Google Public DNS in your TCP/IP settings.

Use the High Performance Power Plan

By default your PC is set to use the Balanced Power option, which will reduce power to non-essential components when not being used. By selecting the High Performance plan your PC will use more power but should run faster all the time. To change the power plan, search for Power Options in the search bar and then click Additional Power Settings > Show Additional Plans.

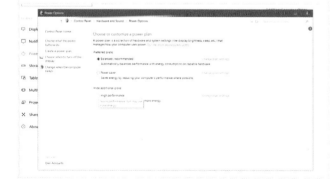

Speed Up Windows Shut Down Time

If you don't mind delving about in the system registry, you can set and adjust the AutoEndTasks, HungAppTimeout, WaitToKillAppTimeout and WaitToKillServiceTimeout values, which control how long Windows waits for hung programs to close, etc. Remember, the registry is very complex and making changes can have a catastrophic effect on your PC.

Uninstall Unneeded Programs

If there are apps or games installed on your system that you just don't use anymore, it's a good idea to uninstall them. This is particularly true of off the shelf PCs that often come preinstalled with a lot of useless software. Fortunately Windows 10 makes this easy, since you can uninstall apps from the Start menu by right-clicking on them and choosing Uninstall from the pop-up menu.

Use the Fast Start-up Option

Windows 10 includes an option to start-up faster by storing an image of the Windows kernel to your hard drive when it shuts down. This saves a lot of time by bypassing a lot of driver loading. In the Power Options, click on 'Choose what power buttons do' and then click 'Change settings that are currently unavailable'. The greyed out settings will become active, including 'Turn on fast start-up'.

Auto Sign in to User Account at Start-up

This is really not recommended for any PC to which others may have access but if you're definitely the only person that will use your PC, you might want to set it so that you don't have to sign in whenever your computer wakes from sleep mode. You can do this in the Accounts > Sign-in options section of the Settings page.

Enable Write Caching for Your Drives

Speed up the performance of your external storage devices by enabling write caching, temporarily storing data in high speed RAM. Right-click on the Start button and open Device Manager. Expand the Disk drives list and double-click on the drive that you want to enable. Click on the Policies tab and you'll see 'Enable write caching on the device' as a check box option.

Stop the Hard Disk Shutting Down

While having your HDDs turn off after a set amount of idle minutes will help save energy, it can also cause your PC to slow down significantly while it waits for the HDD to spin back up. Search for Power Options and you can adjust the idle time to never or just increase the amount of minutes. Alternatively you could install an SSD, which is always at full readiness.

Keep Your PC Tower Clean

Dust can build up inside your machine forming an insulating layer over vital cooling components and reducing their efficiency, which can have an impact on the performance of your system. It's a good idea to open up the case and give it a good clean once in a while. Obviously disconnect it from the mains first, and use a soft brush or a compressed air can to blow dust off the CPU cooling fins, etc.

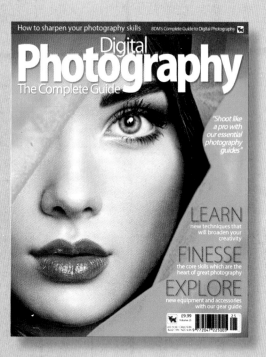
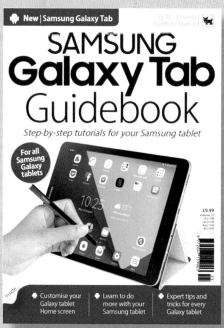
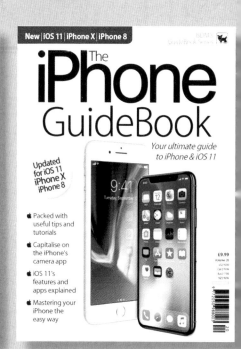

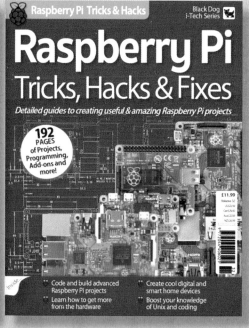